Providence and Free Will in Human Actions

Daniel W. Goodenough

Swedenborg Scientific Association
Bryn Athyn, Pennsylvania
1986

Copyright © 1986 by the Swedenborg Scientific Association

First Edition

ISBN 0-915221-63-2

Library of Congress Catalog Card Number: 86-82261

Cover design by Martha Gyllenhaal of Bryn Athyn, Pennsylvania. The almond-shaped image used in the design, called a mandorla, is a symbol for a glorious sphere. Gold and blue combine to form green, as Providence and free will operate in human actions.

Printed in the United States of America

CONTENTS

FOREWORD

Why did it happen? We ask this question about many events, painful and pleasant, trivial and meaningful. Philosophers, theologians and historians have never agreed on an answer, and the question will always remain an open one.

For those receptive of theistic solutions to the riddles of human life, the question is complicated by the need to reconcile the existence of God with the ever-present reality of evil—however that evil may be defined. No less important is the problem of defining the role people play in human events. Although God is generally conceived of as benevolent and without limitation, the undeniable existence of suffering, catastrophe, and other un-Godlike human experiences seems to belie the infinity of either God's power or His love. And without a definition of God's role, who can understand what function mankind, individually or collectively, has in the course of life? Many believers, especially Christians, have declared God somehow to be the moving force in life and history, and have allowed for little, if any, action that stems from genuinely free human decisions and choices. Despairing of finding a rational, intelligent answer to these timeless dilemmas, many are disposed to "have faith," or place their hope in blind trust in God.

This study is addressed to those who long for more than a blind faith, who wish to find answers which reconcile an almighty and benevolent Divinity with the reality of evil. It is a search for the place of human free will in the drama of life, written for those who from common sense recognize that the life they lead does make a difference, and who believe at the same time that God truly remains in control of His universe. While it would be arrogant to claim that this study presents the definitive answers, I submit that the appropriate questions often are not asked, usually because of an unwillingness to confront squarely the implications of human free will.

The answers I have advanced lie within the context of the theology of the Writings of Emanuel Swedenborg (1688-1772), whose rational, Christian answers to the essential questions of human life remain a treasury largely undiscovered by thoughtful moderns. Where lies the responsibility for the actions and events of the past and of today? The present study attempts to search out whatever can be found in Swedenborg's works to shed light on this question, assuming an almighty God who loves all individuals, and recognizing human experiences as they are.

With the divorce of faith and reason in the late Middle Ages, unified thought disintegrated. The Christian mind was split into a non-reasoning emotional belief, and a scientific, rationalist perspective that did not so much deny God as consider Him irrelevant to the business of life in the world. Following Swedenborg, I believe that God intended real faith to agree with the light of true reason, and that such questions as this study addresses can be answered to the satisfaction of both loving faith and the demands of reason. Failure to seek rational religious answers to the basic philosophical questions of life, relegates the individual and his society to a wasteland without lasting purpose, or even credible solace.

I wish to acknowledge the special work of the personnel of the General Church Press in Bryn Athyn, Pennsylvania. Thanks are due also to Alice Fritz, who tirelessly proofread the text and made helpful suggestions; to my wife Ruth, who typed the original manuscript, proofread the text, and prepared the index; and to Martha Gyllenhaal for her cover design. And I especially wish to thank my colleague Professor Erland Brock, editor of *The New Philosophy*, whose persistent encouragement and attention to detail have succeeded in bringing this study into book form.

Daniel W. Goodenough
Bryn Athyn, Pennsylvania
July 10, 1986

ABBREVIATIONS OF TITLES BY SWEDENBORG

AC	Arcana Coelestia
AE	Apocalypse Explained
AR	Apocalypse Revealed
BE	Brief Exposition
Canons	Canons of the New Church
CL	Conjugial Love
de Conjugio	Concerning Marriage
D Love	Divine Love
D Wis	Divine Wisdom
DLW	Divine Love and Wisdom
DP	Divine Providence
EU	Earths in the Universe
Faith	Doctrine of Faith
HD	New Jerusalem and Its Heavenly Doctrine
HH	Heaven and Its Wonders and Hell
Inv	Invitation to the New Church
ISB	Intercourse of the Soul and the Body
LJ	Last Judgment
PP	Prophets and Psalms
SD	Spiritual Diary
TCR	True Christian Religion

I
The Question

Why do human actions take place as they do? Why have the events in history occurred, instead of other events that might have occurred? Why does each individual act as he does, and not in some other way? What are the causes that produce human action? This study arises from an attempt to answer these questions.[1]

A New Church man's philosophy of life should be based upon the two foundations of truth—the Word, and what he observes in nature.[2] The Word is the foundation itself,[3] and so we begin with the well-known truth that Providence operates in greatest and in least things, in universals and also in the tiniest singulars.[4] The Writings abundantly teach the infinite operation of Providence in every least thing of creation,[5] and these teachings have rightly received considerable emphasis in the New Church. Clearly Providence plays a major role in the cause or determination of human actions. My question is whether it plays the *only* role in causing human actions. Is man free, to some extent, in his natural actions, as he is free in his spirit?

It is important to establish firmly at the outset that whether or not man's actions are freely chosen, it is essentially his mind, not his body, that is free. The essential of freedom is in man's will.[6]

But what does freedom mean? The Writings speak of several different kinds of freedom. Sometimes they refer to the *faculty* of liberty or freedom, and sometimes[7] to man's *use or abuse* of freedom. Every man is given free will, meaning that he can choose good or evil.[8] By his choices he comes into either heavenly freedom or hellish freedom. Heavenly freedom is to follow the Lord and so is freedom itself, while hellish freedom is to follow the lusts that flame up from the hells, and this is really slavery.[9] But for the purposes of this study the important point is that even if man makes bad use of his freedom, he still has free will, or freedom to choose between good and evil. Even if he is on the road to hell, more and more a victim of that apparent freedom which is really slavery to hell, he is still granted the gift of free will; otherwise he would not be able to repent.[10] Even if man is distant from true freedom, the faculty of free will remains with him. It is this faculty of free will, rather than man's use or abuse of freedom, which is at the center of this study, and particularly the question of whether the free will implies some freedom in action.

It is important to establish also that the infinity

and omnipotence of Providence are not at issue. The laws of permission are laws of the Divine Providence,[11] and permissions do not imply an absence or lack of Divine Providence. The first Christian Church has tended to believe that where Providence does not directly cause something, it is therefore absent—and so it appears to the natural man. The existence of permissions has therefore led many to doubt the infinity and universality of Providence.[12] This difficulty is resolved by the doctrine of permissions given in the Writings of Swedenborg, and the question before us is not whether there are permissions, but in what areas of human life they exist. *In what ways* does Providence permit man freely to choose evil? If we say that in Area X Providence permits man to choose evil, this hardly means that Providence is not in operation in Area X. It simply means that one of the modes of Providence is that in Area X it is of order that man shall be free, whether he chooses good or evil.

Does Providence operate by allowing free *actions* as well as free choices of the *will*, or are free actions too dangerous to leave to man's freedom? In either case Providence is infinite and operates in all things. The reasons for permissions are important and will be touched on in the pages that follow, but my principal question revolves around whether permissions extend to human actions.

It should be obvious also that if man does in fact enjoy some freedom in action as well as in mind, that freedom is surely limited—not only by the laws of permission,[13] but also by space and time, and by such factors as heredity, environment, past experiences, and free choices already made. Limitations upon man's freedom are frequently pointed out from religious and secular sources, but such limitations in some area of life do not mean that man has no freedom at all in that area. To the question of limitations on freedom we will also return.

Another important principle to hold in mind is that in all that it does, the Lord's Providence looks to what is infinite and eternal, not to what is finite and temporal.[14] No good is provided that does not look to eternity, nor is any evil permitted that cannot somehow, even if remotely and indirectly, further some eternal end of good.[15] If man is granted some degree of freedom in natural actions, it is not for the sake of the actions themselves or for any temporal purpose, but solely for eternal ends and uses. The natural man may regard free action as a good in itself, but in the Lord's eyes nothing of time or space is good except as it serves an eternal end. The question is whether His eternal ends are served by freedom in man's temporal actions.

A final introductory point concerns the continuing discussion in the New Church about the Lord's foresight and man's freedom. To some the Writings of Swedenborg say that the Lord foresees all things from eternity in the sense that He is aware of all the potential realities, all the potential choices and directions that any and all men may come into. But He does not foresee particular events in the sense that He knows before a human decision is made exactly how it *will* be made.[16] To others the Writings say the Lord does foresee specifically what man will and will not choose; He foresees not simply potentialities but foreknows exactly what choices will be made and foreknows what choices will not be made. I subscribe to the latter interpretation because I believe it is what the plain statements of the Writings directly say;[17] because I see no conflict with the doctrine of free will;[18] and because I believe the alternate interpretation imposes the limitation of time upon the Divine.

The point I wish to make, however, is that the question of *how* the Lord foresees is of only peripheral relevance to the present study. The question before us is not about free choice itself, but whether the free choice which exists in spiritual things exists also in natural actions. In whatever way the Lord foresees, He foresees both spiritual and natural things. Whatever understanding of Divine foresight a man has, presumably applies to both spiritual and natural planes. If the Lord foreknows particular human decisions on the *spiritual* plane, those decisions are still free; and the same would be true on the *natural* plane. But if the Lord does not foreknow the particulars of man's *spiritual* path, then presumably He does not foreknow the particulars of man's *natural* path. Whatever reconciliation a man makes between Divine foresight and human freedom would seem to have little relevance to the question of whether or not that freedom extends into natural actions. (It is interesting to note that of those who tend to see man as free in natural actions, some believe and others disbelieve in Divine foreknowledge of particular decisions; and that those who tend *not* to see man as free in natural actions also represent both interpretations about exactly *how* the Lord foresees.)

II
Why Relevant?

In general, believers in God prefer to think of the course of life as being directed by Providence, such that good always results, nothing really unfair happens, and man's evil is always somehow overruled for good. On the other hand, we feel free in many things, and we want to believe we are free—free to choose good or evil, and therefore responsible for what happens to us and within our spheres of use. It is important to realize that we cannot have it completely both ways, because in the degree that Providence *alone* determines and causes something, man's freedom and responsibility regarding it are eliminated. Man is not responsible for, nor free in regard to, what the Divine alone determines.

Creation of the world, for example, is a completely Divine work, and man is not responsible for how the Lord created the universe. And so Divine creation is altogether good. Where man is free and responsible, however, Providence cannot be the sole cause of something, and the result will not be pure, unmixed good. For instance, Providence permits hell because some men will evil. Providence is not the only cause of hell. Although the laws of Providence constitute one of the reasons that hell exists, another causative factor, without which hell would not exist, is that some men choose to will evil. It is true that it is only from the laws of Providence that man is able to will evil, but that does not mean that Providence is the only cause of hell. Man is one of the causes of hell, and man and his free will must be studied, in addition to the nature of God, before we can understand why the hells exist. Where both Providence and free will cause something, we will find neither unmitigated evil—which Providence cannot allow—nor unmitigated good—since those who are free sometimes choose evil.

Believers in Providence are thus faced with the problem that to the extent man is granted free choice, the course of life is not so directed by Providence that what is best always results. The best will always result only where the Divine alone is operating. Where man is free we can have no assurance that only the best will take place. The causes of a thing matter enormously because they determine whether the thing is all good or has varying degrees of evil in it.

If the causes of natural events are solely from Providence, then natural events are all good when seen interiorly and spiritually, and we need not be greatly concerned about them because our free will cannot affect them; we are not responsible. If free will is partially or sometimes a cause of natural events, then we cannot simply leave natural events to Providence; yet with our responsibility for them goes a lack of assurance that they will all turn out for the best. It matters enormously whether the Divine alone or both the Divine and man are causes of different kinds of spiritual and natural happenings.

For example, we live under the appearance that we are free to affect our children for good or for evil. We *feel* that by cooperating with the Lord we can enable our children to receive more remains from the Lord and a greater distaste for evil than if we do not cooperate with the Lord. New Church education is based upon the assumption that through adults' free response to the Lord some real good can be done for children that would not otherwise be done. Yet at the same time we want to believe that the Lord will so protect and care for the young that no failing of our own will bring harm to them. We feel free to influence our children and want to be able to, and we want also to believe that Providence will allow them to be influenced only for good.

We cannot have it both ways, and if the appearance of freedom is true (in the area of educating and influencing children), then *some* of the responsibility for our children's upbringing and remains from the Lord lies with our free will. If we choose not to make the effort we should, then the remains received will be fewer, and our bad efforts will have a relatively harmful effect. This is how we feel about children who are taught nothing about God or about rejecting evils as sins. Surely Providence sees to it that every child receives some remains, but if Providence is *totally* responsible for the amount and kind of remains that children receive, and for their spiritual upbringing, then the decisions about their children that parents and teachers make daily have no real effect upon their children. Some have felt that the child will receive from the Lord the right amount of remains, however bad his parents are, since it seems unfair to the child if his spiritual background is poor merely on account of his parents. This is a comforting notion, but are we aware that it implies man's educational efforts are irrelevant to his children?

So we cannot have it both ways, even as the Lord could not have a universe without evil and still allow man responsibility for his own destiny. Where Providence alone determines, man's own thought and effort are useless except for his personal contemplation and worship; and where Providence allows some degree of human freedom, man enjoys some responsibility for his actions and their consequences, but must live with the ever-present possibility that the best will not result.

Providence will seek to bring about "the best under the circumstances," but "the best under the circumstances" may contain evil and pain—as for example the hell of the worst profaners, which is surely "the best under the circumstances," but is hardly good.[19] To this subject we will return.

The Lord governs all things, then, but He does not alone decide, determine, or cause all things. (I use *determine,* in the sense of *cause* or *make to happen.)* He reigns over the universe and rules each and everything in it, but in the sense of governing, not in the sense of causing or making to happen.[20] He is the First Cause of all existence,[21] but there are some things of which He is certainly not the cause. He is not responsible for evil.[22] He bends man but does not break him.[23] Thus He does not rule in the sense that He compels.[24] He moderates and arranges all things, and *disposes* them in the sense of arranging, distributing, and setting in order. He *directs* all things in the same sense of arranging and setting in order, but not in the sense of determining. He inflows, purifies and separates; He foresees evil and provides good in every least detail; and He continually accommodates.[25] Does He *control* all things? Certainly, in the sense of *governing* and *arranging,* but not in the sense of *determining* or *causing to happen.* We should use such words as *control, dispose, rule,* and *direct* carefully because today they may connote meanings at variance with their Latin counterparts in the Writings.

It is true that God brings good from both our good and evil efforts. We cannot take the credit when our good efforts result in good, because any good decision we make originates in good from Him. But His use of evil for good ends does not mean that every decision we make is for the best. *True Christian Religion* 504:5 sums up the Lord's government: "God continually holds his finger on the pointer of the balance, regulating but never violating man's free will by compulsion."

If man is to lead his life intelligently, he must come to understand where the human will is granted some free rein, and where the Divine alone is the determining or causative factor. The human tendency is to feel that in the areas close to us (e.g. child-rearing or church government) free will is important and free decisions of man make a difference in what happens. Thus the New Church has zealously stood for freedom in the rearing of children and in school planning and decisions. In areas where we are personally concerned, we tend to demand freedom and to believe we are free and responsible for our effects on others. But in areas in which we are not immediately concerned we may tend to say that the Lord will provide—Providence will see to it that the best happens. Yet it is hardly consistent to believe that free will is a factor in one area, such as child-rearing, and then to say about the economy, or ecology, or a distant war, that whatever happens is for the best. If human choices can make a difference in the education of children, can we say that Providence is the only factor in determining the course of a war? Conversely, if Providence alone determines the historical development of politics, economics and the externals of society, must it not also be the sole cause of everything in those areas of life that are close to our concern? If we believe Providence always causes the best to happen in distant affairs, how rational is it, for example, to pursue reform and change in society close to home?

III
The Traditional Christian View

The foregoing may explain why we should be cautious about the interpretations of Providence and History suggested by religious writers through the ages—that in hidden ways Providence secretly operates such that the final result is always good, whatever the appearance to the contrary. This was the view of many in the first Christian Church, as presented in the early Fifth Century by Augustine of Hippo, and as elaborated by the French Bishop Bossuet in the Seventeenth Century. If history is viewed correctly, said Bossuet, "all iniquities will be corrected, and you will see only wisdom where before you saw disorder."[26] For example, according to Bossuet, all the history of Israel was foreordained by the will of God. Similarly, Roman persecution of the early Christians served the will of God by testing and strengthening the Church, which was in time able to convert Emperor Constantine to Christianity; this in turn transformed pagan Rome into the eternal Rome of true Christianity. It is God alone who forms all kingdoms, "in order to give them to whomsoever He will . . . ."[27] When properly understood, both secular and ecclesiastical history must be explained not by mere historical and particular causes, but by the secret ordering of God.

Bossuet is the kind of writer who at first glance, people are inclined to say, seems to be very close to New Church thinking. The specific teachings of the Writings about the history of Israel are somewhat similar to Bossuet's,[28] and many New Church men have seen in the ancient Roman Empire uses close to those suggested by Bossuet.[29] This traditional Christian view of Providence and history has met with some favor among New Church men, although not in all particulars. It is a reassuring interpretation, offering confidence during even the worst moments of natural life and history. It affirms that Providence does all things, yet it allows for free will and choice in spiritual things, even if not in natural things. It is comforting to believe that Providence so controls the course of human events that all apparent evil is really good.

Both the Writings of Swedenborg and experience may seem to confirm the traditional Christian view. The Writings stress that man's real freedom is in *spiritual* things, and they often note limitations upon freedom of action.[30] And if the end, love, or intention, rather than the deed, is the man himself,[31] is it not enough that man be free to choose his intentions and ends? Need he be free to carry them out in action? Some passages seem to say that Providence bestows or withholds worldly success and prosperity according to man's spiritual need—that is, that his spiritual state rather than his natural activity is what determines the degree of his worldly prosperity.[32] The implication would be that natural action matters little, since everything important is decided purely on the plane of the spirit—that is, natural actions are determined by Providence, while man is free only in his spirit.

Secular studies of the mind have also concluded at great length that many of our supposedly free actions in fact result from psychological conditioning and various other factors, many of them unconscious. Much modern psychological theory furthers the concept of man as not truly free in the decisions he consciously makes in natural life. Perhaps, it has been suggested in the New Church, man is not free except in the innermost recesses of his mind, deep within his spirit. Cannot man be internally free in his spirit to choose good or evil even while a great many of his external activities and habits are determined for him, apparently by external psychological causes but secretly by Providence?

In an age which abounds in serious abuse of freedom we are perhaps inclined to emphasize the doctrines of Providence, order, and authority.

Surely one of the greatest failures of our time is the loss of any real sense of order, on account of a rejection of ultimate authority. Concerning this, much has been and should be said. The present may hardly seem a good time to lay too much stress on free will, of which we may even be a little afraid. Nearly everyone must admit that to contemplate the free will as having any real effect on the direction and course of man, society, and history is terrifying. In sum, the appeals of Bossuet's interpretation of history and life are considerable, promising apparent agreement with both revelation and psychological experience even while the troubled spirit is assured that things are really all for the good.

IV
What Do the Writings Say?

Disturbing as it may be, the question must be asked—how free is man to influence the external things of life, other people, the course of history, the future of the Church? What, if any, is his role in causing things to happen? For a number of reasons I find the traditional Christian view, while holding an essential kernel of truth, seriously deficient when examined in the light of the Writings and of common sense. The kernel of truth lies in the principle that an infinite and benevolent Providence, looking to eternity, does operate continually in all things from greatest to least, from firsts to lasts; and that from understanding this infinite government some Divine direction of life and history, some Divine order and purpose in external events, may be seen.[33]

As a total philosophy of life and history, however, the interpretation that Providence alone determines the course of natural life and history fails most seriously. To begin with, the traditional interpretation simply reflects the Old Jewish and Christian idea that if God does not Himself determine all things, then His government is finite and limited. But the New Church idea of Divine government is far more involved than the notion that the Lord causes all things to happen. For that idea we need resort only to Bossuet and other Christian writers, and would not need the many teachings revealed in the Writings concerning the operation of Providence.

More fundamentally, if natural actions were not free, but were determined by Providence, then natural life would be in order. Any evil in the natural events of life can come not from God but only from free choices of evil by man. Now there certainly does appear to be evil in natural life; man frequently appears to produce evil in action. But we can never judge with certainty about a specific human act, that it is interiorly evil stemming from a free choice of evil[34] Yet the appearance is very strong, around us and within our own actions, that when we choose to be moved by evil, we often express that choice by freely *doing* evil.

Is this appearance correct? It can be argued that apparent evil deeds are not freely done, that man does not really decide to do them, that Providence alone secretly sees to it that an apparently evil action is done for the sake of some good, and thus that apparent evil action is really good when properly understood. Is apparent evil action really evil, freely chosen by man, or is it in fact interiorly good, the work of Providence?

The Writings reply plainly that much human action is indeed evil, and that free spiritual choices of evil not always, but often, involve natural *actions* and spoken *words* that also are evil, not secretly good. For instance *True Christian Religion* 479, in proving that man has free will in *spiritual* things, lists a number of *natural human events,* some from the Word, some from history. The last six examples are as follows:

> 7, [The Jewish] nation was at length permitted to establish a religious system in many respects not in conformity with the Sacred Scripture. 8, The Christian religion is divided into many sects, and each of them is riven by heresies. 9, There are so many impious people in the Christian world and so much glorying in impiety; and also plots and strategems contrived against the pious, the just and the upright. 10, Injustice prevails over justice in the law courts and in business. 11, The impious also are exalted to honors and become great men and leaders. 12, Wars are permitted, in which there is so much slaughter of men and ravaging of cities, nations and families; and so on.

The passage then concludes: "Is it possible to account for such things except from the fact that every man has free will?"

Clearly all these examples result from spiritual choices of evil. *True Christian Religion* 479 thus shows that free will has effects in the natural universe, and that part of the Lord's rule involves permitting actual evils in external life—evils that He does not will, but that result from man's free will. *Divine Providence* 234-274 goes over the same examples and shows specifically why they have been permitted, and why the things that are permitted are not as bad as what would happen if they were not permitted. But neither the *True Christian Religion* nor *Divine Providence* passages say that these events were really interiorly good. Rather they show they were evil, from man's abuse of free will. Thus the teaching emerges that man has *some* real freedom in his actions.

The example of injustice prevailing over justice in law courts and business[35] also indicates that a man's worldly success is not always according to his inner spiritual need. When studied carefully, *Arcana Coelestia* 8717 shows that *if a man is in good,* then riches and honors are given him according to his spiritual need.[36] But for the evil, honors and riches may be "stumbling blocks" to true worship[37] and in fact "curses."[38] Honors and wealth "may be blessings and may also be curses, and . . . when they are blessings they are from God, and when they are curses they are from the devil. Moreover, it is well-known that honors and wealth are bestowed by the devil, for from this he is called the prince of the world."[39] "When eminence and riches do not lead astray they are from God, but when they do they are from hell."[40]

The implication is that with the evil, honors and riches are not distributed according to spiritual need. The good are given the right amount of worldly prosperity and success for their spiritual state, while to the evil, wealth and honors are curses rather than blessings because they lead away from the life of heaven. Nor do the Writings reject the appearance that cunning and deceit are means to unjust success in the world.[41] Thus some men are seduced by riches and drawn away from heaven.[42] Swedenborg found in heaven many who had been wealthy on earth from business and trade, "but not so many of those who were in stations of honor and became rich through their offices; and for the reason that these latter by the gains and honors that resulted from their dispensing justice and equity, and also by the lucrative and honorable positions bestowed on them, were led into loving themselves and the world. . . ."[43] In other words, man's acquisition of wealth, honors and power on earth may be evil or good; and if it can sometimes be evil, then there must be some degree of freedom in man's natural actions.

Other examples of evil in ultimates include the teaching of *Conjugial Love* 460 and 502-504 that the act of defloration apart from the end of marriage brings a woman into a spiritual state of unchastity, lust and whoredom (unless, presumably, she repents). *Conjugial Love* 502 also shows that the kind of information young women acquire about physical sex affects their state of chastity. *Conjugial Love* has a number of examples of natural evils which would make no sense unless man had some freedom in his actions.

One of the most striking examples of an ultimate, natural evil is given in *Heaven and Hell* 344. Through Swedenborg's eyes good spirits and angels saw little boys fighting in a city, being encouraged by parents and bystanders. The good spirits and angels

> were so revolted at it that I felt their horror, and especially that parents should incite their children to such things, saying that in this way parents extinguish in the earliest age all the mutual love and all the innocence that little children have from the Lord, and initiate them into hatred and revenge. Consequently by their own endeavors they shut their children out of heaven, where there is nothing but mutual love. Let parents therefore who wish well to their children beware of such things.

This can scarcely mean that parents can literally condemn their children to hell. But if parents can in any sense even temporarily "shut their children out of heaven," they clearly have some real spiritual effect on their children. And it should be obvious that this example of natural evil is a further indication of freedom in human action.

The history of Israel provides many specific instances of evil actions which were permitted for various uses but which were still evil. For example, the slaughter of the Shechemites[44] was allowed so that a good would be served. But this does not mean the slaughter was good. It was "an enormous crime.... When any such crime is permitted by the Lord, it is evil men and their infernal instigators who are the authors of it."[45] If the Shechemites had continued to live, it is true that even worse evil would have resulted, so that from their point of view the slaughter was a lesser evil, in fact better than something worse that endangered them. It may have been the best thing under the circumstances, although the Writings do not quite say that. Maybe the *best* under the circumstances would have been something else which neither the sons of Jacob, the Shechemites, or anyone else chose to do. The slaughter was still an evil, and would never have been necessary either if the sons of Jacob had not been present with them, or if the sons of Jacob (and many, many generations of men before them since the Most Ancient Church) had not freely chosen to become external, natural men.[46]

When the "best under the circumstances" is an evil, in other words, it is because prior free choices of evil have resulted in a situation of such appalling evil and disorder that only further permission of evil can avoid a worse evil.[47] We should look for the good for which evils are permitted, yet never forget that permissions are permissions *of evil,* and would not have become necessary if earlier choices of evil, and a general situation of evil, had not arisen. When an evil man rages helplessly against good, rather than overtly harming others, or when a man loses his temper and curses bitterly to himself rather than striking out violently against his friends, perhaps what happens is the best under the evil circumstances, but it is still an evil. Such evil words and actions are not interiorly goods willed by God; they are caused at least partly by evil choices of men. "When any such crime [as the slaughter of the Shechemites] is permitted by the Lord, it is evil men and their infernal instigators who are the author of it"—not God.[48]

Moreover, the actual *doing* of evil worsens its spiritual hold upon man.[49] The intention is the man himself, but if man then carries out the intention, he brings the love and its delights more strongly into himself.[50] If actual doing of an evil can make it worse in man, is it not obvious that the doing of it must be from man and his freedom, and not from the Lord?[51]

While many more examples of actual natural evil could be cited from the history of Israel, one further teaching should be mentioned—that "the Word was changed on account of that nation, as to its external sense, not as to its internal sense."[52] "The sense of the letter of the Word would have been different if the Word had been written among a different people, or if that people had not been such as it was."[53] The examples given[54] make clear that the evil actions to which the Israelites were prone caused the Word to be written differently in the letter than it might have been. This teaching would make no sense if man did not have some freedom in natural actions to do evil.

The Lord said to His followers: "Woe unto the world because of offences! for it must needs be that offences come; but woe to that man by whom the offence cometh!"[55] Though this passage is not expounded directly in the Writings, from the foregoing we can see in what sense "it must needs be that offences come . . . . " Offences can hardly be of any Divine necessity.[56] In the Old Testament evils are ascribed to the Lord, since in no other way could He be believed omnipotent.[57] The Lord's disciples may have understood Matthew 18:7 as meaning that Jehovah God sent the offences, by causing man to do them.[58] But in the light of the teachings about the origin of evil natural actions, we should rise above the appearances of the Old Testament letter and realize that from Jehovah God can come no evil. He wills no offences, and they "must needs" come solely because man wills them. The Lord's words refer not to Divine necessity but to a fact of life—a fact necessitated by the evils within the human race. The Writings speak of the same necessity of offences coming in countless passages about permission, such as *Divine Providence* 251. That it is solely man's evil that make offences necessary appears clearly from the wording in a parallel passage in Luke: "It is impossible but that offences will come; but woe unto him through whom they come!"[59] "Impossible but that" implies something unavoidable, but hardly willed.

V
Freedom to Do

Nor do the Writings merely give man examples of evil natural actions. They also teach in plain statements that to some extent at least man is free in his words and deeds. "It is granted to man *to act* from the freedom of reason, to the end that good may be provided for him, and this is why man has the freedom to think and will even what is evil, *and to do it* so far as the laws do not forbid."[60] Man "is able to will *and to do* what he thinks . . . ."[61] The evil on earth are given "successes" according to their "projects."[62] More forcefully we are taught:

> The evil succeed according to their skill, because it is in agreement with order that everyone should do what he does from reason, and also from freedom; and unless, therefore, it were left to men to act according to reason from freedom, *and thus also unless the actions proceeding therefrom succeeded,* men could in no way be brought to receive eternal life. . . . Nothing which is done from compulsion cleaves to a man, for it is not his. That becomes the man's own which is done from freedom; for that which is from the will is done from freedom, and the will

> is the man himself. Unless, therefore, a man were kept in freedom *to do evil,* good could not be provided for him by the Lord.[63]

The next number presents a concise definition of permission: "To leave a man from his freedom *to do* evil also, is called permission."[64] When this number is read in the context of *Arcana Coelestia* 10777, it makes clear that the *principal* use of permission is that man may be in freedom. Without freedom *to do* evil, the passage is saying, man would not be in the freedom he must be in, in order to be saved. *That* is the principal reason there are permissions. But what is permitted is evil, not a secret good. The good that is within permission lies chiefly in the fact that the evildoer remains in freedom to be saved. There are many other goods which can emerge out of evil, but the primary good seems to be the continuation of man's freedom.

These passages all put emphasis on man's freedom *to do* as well as *to will and think.* This hardly implies that man's free choice is essentially a freedom of action. We have already seen that in essence freedom is freedom to will and think. But the teachings on freedom *in doing* show that we must examine carefully the doctrine that man is free *in spiritual things.*[65] The "spiritual things" in which man is free refer not just to mental things, but to "such things as concern salvation and eternal life."[66] As we shall see, and as common sense perceives, *doing* as well as *willing* and *thinking* have a great deal to do with "salvation and eternal life." The "spiritual things" in which man is free embrace the totality of his spiritual and natural existence.

Thus the "internal man" that is free is not a deep, interior plane of which man is not conscious. The internal man that is free means man's real will—the real man as he acts and speaks "in the company of his intimate friends," as opposed to the external man that acts and speaks "before the world."[67] The man as he is with his close friends, or "at home and left to himself"[68]—this is the internal man that is free. This internal man we can and should be conscious of, to some extent at least. The term *internal man* is used in many different ways in the Writings, and it is always important to let context define an individual term. The point here is that in teaching that it is the internal man that is free, the Writings mean not a hidden, unconscious plane of the mind; they simply mean the real man, as opposed to the fronts he assumes in the company of others.

It is because of the connection of mental and natural life that Divine revelation does not merely inveigh against evil willing and thinking, but also against evil *doing*. That man should shun not only evil willing but also evil doing implies that he is free in his actions. "The Lord in a thousand passages in the Word has taught that man must do good and must not do evil, and this the Lord would by no means have said unless something had been given to man by which he has the ability to do . . . ."[69] *True Christian Religion* 483 reiterates this point, again with considerable stress upon deeds. "What would be the use of all this [the commands to do good and not to do evils] if man had no free will in spiritual things, that is, in such things as concern salvation and eternal life?"[70] In the words of a good spirit, "Of what use, then, would the Word be if a man had no power to will and think *and consequently to do and say* what is there commanded? If man had not this power, religion and the church would be like a wrecked ship lying on the bottom of the sea . . . ."[71]

This teaching on repentance is frequently echoed. Repentance in its essence consists of such mental activities as seeing evils in oneself, acknowledging them, then not willing them, and finally holding them in aversion.[72] But is it not obvious that these essentially mental processes involve actions as well—*not doing* what one had been doing previously? The chapter on repentance in the *True Christian Religion* is very difficult to understand without a giving up of evil actions as well as evil intentions. For example, *True Christian Religion* 535-536 teach about "an easier kind of repentance": man repents if he simply sees that a thing he wants to do is evil and says to himself, "I am thinking of this, and intending it; but as it is a sin, I will not *do* it."[73]

Are not such teachings on repentance meaningless unless man has some freedom in his actions? The Old Testament, the New Testament, and the Writings continually command us to shun evil action and to perform good actions. The emphasis in the latter two shifts away from the Old Testament stress upon actions alone, but the primacy of the life and freedom of the spirit should not seduce us into thinking the life and freedom of the body is irrelevant.

Similarly the doctrine of use emphasizes greatly the actual doing of works of charity. A full consideration of the spiritual and natural elements of use is beyond our present scope, but let us note well that commands to use are commands to actions as well as to spiritual affections. Charity is in essence a *willing* well to the neighbor, but the chapter on Charity in the *True Christian Religion* makes abundantly clear that *acting* well towards the neighbor is also part of charity.[74] Use is more than just doing, but it cannot be separated from doing. Many passages about use speak of *performing* uses and *shunning idleness* as the devil's pillow. Man's "earthly body has been formed to serve the understanding and the will in the world, and to perform uses in conformity with them in the ultimate sphere of nature."[75] "By uses are meant the uses of each one's function, which are the uses of his office, pursuit and occupation. In the Lord's sight these uses are good works themselves."[76] "Use is to perform one's office and to do one's work rightly, faithfully, sincerely, and justly."[77] "Doing truths is performing uses."[78] In their beginnings uses are "truths of doctrine" (that bears considerable reflection); "but in their progression they become goods; they become goods *when the man acts according to these truths. Thus the action itself gives quality to truths,* for all action descends from the will...."[79] It is *the will* that turns truth into good, but action is an essential step in the process.

Many more passages might be cited concerning the importance of *doing* good works and *performing* uses. Surely it must follow that man is gifted with freedom to do or not do the uses he is supposed to perform.

VI
Organic Unity of Man

"The action itself gives quality to truths...."[80] Man is a connected whole, not a series of unrelated mental and physical planes. The body and spirit are inextricably interwoven, and so also are the freedom of the spirit and the freedom of the body. Because the will is free, the body also enjoys freedom.

> Consider also, whatever your circumstances may be, whether without free will you can think at all; and whether in your conversation, in your prayers to God, in preaching and even in listening, free will does not operate at every point. Indeed, without free will even in the most minute particulars, you would no more breathe than a statue....[81]

> It is not denied that a man has free will in natural things; but he enjoys this as a consequence of his free will in spiritual things.[82]

> The Lord keeps man in freedom of thought, and so far as external bonds, such as fear of the law and of life, and fear of the loss of reputation, honor and gain do not prevent, He keeps man in freedom of action.[83]

> All that is called *freedom* which belongs to the will, and thus which belongs to love. On this ground it is that freedom manifests itself through the delight of willing and thinking, and hence that of doing and speaking . . . .[84]

Other passages similarly stress the unity of freedom of spirit and body.

> Free will in spiritual things, being the source of all this freedom, is thus imparted to all forms of free will in natural things; and by means of these the love ruling in the highest regions assumes whatever is conducive to its purposes. The communication between spiritual and natural freedom is like the channel between the fountain and the waters that are fed from it, and like that between the prolific principle in the seed and every single part of the tree, particularly the fruit, in which it is reproduced.[85]

We should note especially the organic unity between the fountain and stream, and between the seed and the tree: without a tree, the seed (analogous to freedom in spiritual things) dies useless.

Thus there is an organic unity of man, and of freedom in spiritual and natural things. Will and action are closely related.

> Free will resides in a man's soul in the fullest perfection; and thence, as the spring water into the fountain, it flows into the two parts of his

> mind, the will and the understanding, and through these into the bodily senses, and into speech and action. For there are in every man three degrees of life, the soul, the mind, and the sensual body; and whatever is in a higher degree is in a state of perfection above that which is in a lower degree. This freedom is the means by which, in which and with which the Lord is present with man, unceasingly urging to be received.[86]

Freedom is in its perfection in the interiors of man, but it is also present in his lower degrees, though in a less perfect state. Anyone can observe that he is more free in his thoughts and affections than in his words and actions. Again, we read in *True Christian Religion* 489: "What is free will but man's power to will and to act, to think and to speak to all appearances as from himself?" Note the close tie between will and action, and between thinking and speaking.

There is a considerable body of doctrine to explain the connection of will and action, or of spirit and body, and a study of this scope can do no more than survey the most cogent teachings. The doctrines of spiritual and natural substance, discrete degrees, influx and correspondences are all relevant, as is the doctrine of instrumental causes and ultimates. In many passages the Writings stress that for will to be will, it must be carried into action. "The mind, in the very act of operating, acts together with and at the same time as the body."[87] The soul and body act as one in operation.[88]

A particularly important sequence is *Divine Love and Wisdom* 215-220, from which I quote only the following:

> It is according to angelic wisdom that unless the will and understanding, that is, affection and thought, as well as charity and faith, clothe and wrap themselves in works or deeds, whenever possible, they are only like something airy which passes away, or like phantoms in air which perish; and that *they first become permanent in man and a part of his life, when he practices and does them.* The reason is that the ultimate is the complex, containant and base of things prior.[89]

Elsewhere we read:

> *To love the Lord* means to do uses from Him and for His sake.... Loving these is doing them, for what a man loves he does. No one can love the Lord in any other way.... Love, unless it becomes deed, ceases to be love, since deed is the bringing about of its purpose, and is that in which it has its existence.... A man's mind, in each separate part of it, extends into all things of his body; it is into all things of the body that its range of activity is, for it is the very form of life. Unless the mind had that field, there would not be a mind, not a man. It is in consequence of the above that the choice and good pleasure of a man's will instantly bring forth and determine actions....[90]

Many passages describe how affection and thought flow into action and speech. "By creation there are gestures corresponding to every affection, and a man falls into them spontaneously when he comes into the affection, provided he has not learned to counterfeit affections that are foreign to him. . . ."[91] The body is nothing but obedience to the mind;[92] and when man "wills to do this or that, in this manner or that, and is thinking of it, the organs then move in concurrence, thus in accordance with the intention of the function or use. . . ."[93]

> The mind actuates the body in externals, and generally in response to its every suggestion. It moves the eye to see, the ears to hear, the mouth and tongue to speak, the hands to act, the feet to walk, the generative organs to propagate. The mind moves not only the externals to these actions but also the internals throughout the whole series, the last from the inmost and the inmost from the last. Thus while it is moving the mouth to speak, it at the same time moves the lungs, the larynx, the glottis, the tongue, the lips, each separately to its own function, and even the face to present a suitable expression.[94]

Would any of this be possible if actions were not free?

The principle which governs the body's acting from will and understanding is the law of correspondences.[95] In other words, not any gesture or action will clothe a particular affection or thought, for the ultimates of the body correspond to the will and understanding. "Those things which from the thoughts are determined into speech, and those which from the will are determined into acts in the body, flow in an orderly way [*ordinate*] into act by general influx, according to correspondences with the Grand Man . . . ."[96]

Swedenborg wondered why particular spirits did not govern speech and action as well as thought and will. "But I was instructed that speech follows from thought, and action from will, and that this flows from order, thus through general influx . . . ."[97] "When thought is determined into speech, and voluntary things into action, the determination and transition into the body are according to order, and are not ruled by any spirits in particular . . . ."[98] If spirits could rule man's speech and action, they would possess his body.[99] In other words, the Lord carefully governs spirits so that affection and thought will not be prevented from being expressed in word and deed. This does not mean the body is as free as the spirit, because there are some restraints upon speech and action. But clearly man has been created so that the body can carry into act and speech what the spirit wills and thinks.

Why is this? The fundamental reason man is at

least somewhat free in action as well as on the plane of the spirit is that the spiritual cannot be without the natural for its existence or standing forth. It is the plane of nature that provides a necessary ultimate basis for the spiritual. Again, a full presentation of this doctrine would lengthen this study well beyond its usefulness, but a few important passages must be cited.

The spiritual world cannot stand forth or subsist without the natural world.[100] Can the spiritual nevertheless *be* without the natural, even if it cannot *stand forth* alone? No, because *esse* and *existere* cannot be separated. "*Esse* is not *esse* unless it *stands forth,* because prior to this it is not in a form, it has no quality, and that which has no quality is not anything."[101] "*Esse* is nothing unless it stands forth; and it becomes something by standing forth."[102] Where there is a first, there must be a last, or ultimate.[103] "Divine order never subsists in the middle, and there forms something without an ultimate, for it is not in its fullness and perfection; but it proceeds to the ultimate; and when it is in its ultimate, then it forms, and by means collected there it renews itself and produces itself further . . . ."[104]

We may ask why this is so. Is not the spiritual real and substantial? It is, but in a different way from natural substance. Unlike natural things, spiritual things are not fixed and static; in fact their lack of fixity constitutes the difference between the spiritual and natural universes.[105] Spiritual things of themselves are not permanent or constant.[106] Of themselves spiritual things are continually shifting and changing. This is why no procreations of men are possible except in the ultimates of nature,[107] and why man could not survive without a limbus or border drawn from the finest things of nature.[108] Were he separated from this ultimate, "his spiritual things, which belong to the thoughts and affections of his spirit, would flow away, like things unfounded."[109]

The impermanence of spiritual things may be seen by anyone from reflection upon his own shifting affections and thoughts; these become permanent in him according as he acts from them. All spiritual things—love and wisdom, will and understanding, affection and thought—become permanent by being clothed in natural ultimates, and until then they are perpetually changing their state. The road to hell is paved not with actual good intentions, but with temporary feelings of good will that are lost in the shuffle because they are not carried into action.

Hence we have the doctrine of ultimates: the Lord's operation in man and creation is not from firsts through mediates into ultimates, "but from firsts through ultimates and thus into mediates."[110] "Where there is a first there must always be an ultimate, and . . . everything intermediate from the first exists together in the ultimate . . . ."[111]

A good example of the importance of ultimates is given in the treatment of national genius found in *True Christian Religion* 813-815, where it is shown that the degree of spiritual enlightenment a nation enjoys is affected by the degree of civil freedom it has.[112]

The doctrine of instrumental causes reinforces the point.

> Both an active and a *passive* are necessary to every operation, and . . . nothing can be produced from an *active* alone, and nothing from a *passive* alone. It is similar with what is spiritual and what is natural; what is spiritual, as a living force, being active, and what is natural, as a dead force, being passive . . . . In every effect which is produced there are both a principal and an instrumental cause, and . . . these two, when anything is done, appear as one, although they are distinctly two; wherefore it is one of the laws of wisdom that the principal and the instrumental cause make together one cause: so also do what is spiritual and what is natural.[113]

Thus "the varied can stand forth only in what is constant, fixed and certain."[114] Without a fixed foundation angels would disappear, just as visible spiritual things disappear when the angelic affections to which they correspond are changed.[115] It is the use of the natural to provide fixation for what is alive—to give the spiritual a foundation of constancy so that it may stand forth and subsist. Nature was created in order that "in ultimates all things may be fixed, settled and constant, and that thence there may stand forth things which are permanent and durable: thus and no otherwise is creation founded."[116]

The means of creation, then, are discrete degrees which in themselves are separated from each other. But creation, and man, do not consist of isolated planes of reality which do not communicate with each other. (This would be so if man were free only in his interior planes and not in his conscious life and actions.) Discrete degrees communicate with each other through influx and correspondences, and in this way there is an overall connection of everything created, from firsts to ultimates.[117] It is by means of discrete degrees in all things that the created universe is a connected and coherent whole.[118] Thus all things of man's spirit and body are held in "continuous connection."[119] If everything from firsts to lasts were not so held in continuous connection, they would cease to be; "what is unconnected is dissipated as nothing."[120] All planes of creation are connected and all planes of man are connected. Life is solely from the spiritual, not from the natural, but neither the spiritual nor the natural can survive without connection to the other.

This is the reason that the actions of the body are so important, and that the Lord could not give man a freedom of the spirit without granting him also a freedom of bodily action. Stated simply, man does not choose good and evil abstractly from day-to-day life. He chooses good or evil in the decisions he makes daily in meeting the actual challenges and problems that confront him. It matters *spiritually* what he does in his physical actions right here, now. Although good external actions do not necessarily mean he has made good spiritual choices, a spiritual choice, before it really is a spiritual choice, must be carried out in some kind of corresponding action. Hence the necessity of some freedom of action. Even the formation of an intention, I believe, must involve some physical activity, however small; and of course if an intention is not acted upon when there is opportunity, it is not a true intention, but a passing affection and thought.[121] "To will is to love doing."[122] "For unless a man does that which he wills there is within him the failure to will which eventually becomes lack of will."[123] If spiritual choices do not need to be carried out in some degree of natural freedom, why do we bother?

There is even the remarkable statement, *"Act precedes, man's willing follows;* for that which a man does from the understanding, he *at last* does from the will, and *finally* puts it on as a habit; and it is *then* insinuated in his rational or internal man. And when it has been insinuated in this, the man no longer does good from truth, but from good . . . ."[124] Action is thus necessary for truth to become good in man. The teaching that "the action itself gives quality to truths"[125] (AC 4984) is not a passing comment, but essential for our understanding of the very meaning and purpose of our human existence.

VII
Is Man's Freedom Contingent on Others?

An important question arises if man is free in speech and action as well as in mind: how much real effect can he have upon other people? Can he affect their spiritual state in any lasting way? Or does Providence so regulate the interiors of all men that no one's decisions will have any permanent spiritual effects on others?

Again, we cannot have it both ways, since if through our free choices we can have a good effect on another, such that his spiritual life is permanently helped in some way it would not otherwise be helped, then it follows that we can also have bad effects on others—if in no other way, then by *not* having a possible good effect on him. On the other hand, if Providence so carefully regulates man's states that nothing we choose to say or do can be harmful to another in any lasting way, then it follows that however much the Lord may use us for good, our own free efforts will have no real effects on another and his eternal spiritual life will be the same whatever we do. We may instinctively rebel at this dilemma, desiring both providential protection of man from any harm, and also the ability to have effects for eternal good upon our neighbor.

In an earlier part of the study (WHAT DO THE WRITINGS SAY?) several examples from the Writings were presented which indicate that man can have permanent spiritual effects on others by his freely chosen actions. To take a few specific instances, parents can "extinguish in the earliest age all the mutual love and all the innocence that little children have from the Lord, and initiate them into hatred and revenge. Consequently by their own endeavors they shut their children out of heaven . . . ."[126] At least so the angels told Swedenborg. If someone had said, "But the Lord will protect them; He would not permit bad parents to bring any lasting harm to their children", would the angels have felt differently? Perhaps, yet the passage suggests otherwise, speaking not of providential prevention of any harm being done, but of their horror at what some parents did. "Let parents therefore who wish well to their children beware of such things." The angels did not say parents can grant or withhold salvation, but they clearly thought that parents can have major spiritual effects on their children.[127]

A similar conclusion emerges from the teachings on defloration.[128] After the door of conjugial love has been broken through, if she does not repent "a woman deflowered by such men loses her modesty and becomes a harlot, and *of this that robber also is the cause.*"[129] This hardly exonerates the woman from responsibility, but it seems clear that the man is partly a cause of the spiritual state into which such a woman comes. (This is a major theme of Leo Tolstoy's novel, *Resurrection. Arcana Coelestia* 1113 presents a similar example.)

Again, nuns, priests and monks are released after death from their vows of celibacy, but some of these who are good choose to remain celibate and live at the sides of heaven.[130] The doctrine of celibacy has had eternal effects upon their spiritual life. It is clear that their own free response to that doctrine determines their eternal homes, but have not the previous decisions of countless people who developed the dogma of celibacy in the first place had a real, permanent influence on the spiritual lives of such celibates? Had they not lived in a society that highly valued celibacy, would they now be at the sides of heaven? The case for man's having *some* spiritual effect upon others seems strong.

Finally, the slaughter of the Shechemites very clearly had spiritual effects upon the Shechemites—good effects in this case.[131] Protection from profanation was one of the reasons the Lord permitted the Shechemites to be destroyed.

But the slaughter was not the work of the Lord; it was the work of the sons of Israel, as the Writings make very plain.[132] Here again we see men's free decisions—the decision to slaughter the Shechemites and many past decisions which brought about the evil situation in the first place—seem to be able to have some eternal consequences for other people.

Now man's eternal home results from the man's own free decisions. No influence we can have on another can send him permanently to any society of heaven or hell where he does not choose to be. In that sense a man's freedom is not contingent upon anyone else's free decisions. Yet from these and other examples it appears that the decisions of one man may inhibit or limit the freedom of others to some extent.

Probably the fullest discussion of this question is in *Divine Providence* 129-153. Here it is shown that states of mind do occur in which free will is not entirely destroyed, but neither is a man free to be reformed and regenerated. Some of these states come from such things as sickness, insanity, and misfortune. Others come from self-justification and various fears or evil within the man himself. But some such states arise from the decisions of other men—such as compulsion to worship. Human choice is the source of some of the non-free states in which others can not be reformed.

Now with all such states the internal remains free and uncompelled.[133] "Fear can in no wise invade the internal of thought, this being always in freedom because it is his life's love . . . ."[134] "No one can be compelled to believe contrary to what he thinks in his heart to be true."[135] Hence we have the frequent teaching that man's spiritual freedom is never violated.[136]

But the doctrine does not rest here. Although compulsion cannot invade the internal of man, this does not mean that man can never impede another's free choice in spiritual things. The *internal* cannot be forced to change, but if the *external* is not free, the man is not free to be reformed. The passage just quoted (teaching that fear can in no way invade the internal of thought) continues that fear "can invade the external of thought, and when it does this the internal of thought is closed; and when this is closed man can no longer act from freedom according to his reason, and therefore cannot be reformed."[137] The body may be compelled, indeed to some extent it should be.[138] "But the external of his spirit, which consists in thinking and willing, must not be compelled, for *thus perishes his internal freedom by which he is reformed.*"[139] "Free will really belongs to the internal man; and when this is closed up, the man becomes external and natural; and such a man does not see any spiritual truth."[140]

In other words, the internal of man always

remains free in that it is not changed by fear or compulsion, but neither can it change itself without flowing into the external. The internal will and thought cannot function in isolation on their own plane, apart from the external will and thought and to some extent the body. "Everything of the understanding and of the will must be formed by means of the external before it is formed by means of the internal."[141]

> The state of man's thought is such that from the internal of his thought he sees a thing in the external of his thought as in a kind of mirror. . . . When he sees the thing, as in mirror, he can also turn it this way and that, and shape it until it appears to him to be a thing of beauty. If this is a truth it may be compared to a maiden or a youth, beautiful and living. If, however, the man cannot turn it this way and that and shape it, but can only believe it from the persuasion induced by a miracle, it may be compared, if it is then a truth, to a maiden or a youth carved from stone or wood, in which there is no life. It may also be compared to an object that is constantly before the sight and, being alone seen, hides from view everything that is on either side of it and behind it. Again, it may be compared to a continual sound in the ear that takes away the perception of harmony arising from many sounds. Such blindness and deafness are induced on the human mind by miracles. *It is the same with everything that is confirmed which is not seen with some degree of rationality before being confirmed.*[142]

The immediate reference in this passage is to persuasive faith induced by miracles, but the last sentence and the argument throughout the passage make clear that anything that compels the external of thought deprives man of liberty and rationality by preventing the Lord from flowing in "through the internal into the external of thought."[143]

Thus we are taught that the internal, even though its own freedom is inviolate,

> is so averse to compulsion by the external that it turns itself away. This is because the internal wishes to be in freedom, and loves freedom, for freedom belongs to the love or life of man.... Therefore when freedom feels itself being compelled *it withdraws as it were within itself and turns itself away,* and regards compulsion as an enemy; for the love that constitutes the life of man is irritated and causes the man to think that in this matter he is not master of himself, and consequently that his life is not his own.... From this it is clear that it is harmful to compel men to Divine worship by threats and punishments.[144]

Compulsion cannot change the internal, but it limits and restricts it, and by boxing it into itself (*closing* it, *Divine Providence* 139:2), prevents the man as a whole from freely choosing to be reformed. The man himself then feels he is not his own master because the internal cannot flow into an external that is forced and rigid; it can just survive within itself until restraints are removed. Anyone can attest to this who remembers a state in which his freedom was seriously challenged by compulsion.

The essence of man, then, is his *internal* will and understanding, but in order to exercise free will in spiritual things—to change, compel oneself, repent, be reformed, or sink deeper into the love of evil—the man must be able to operate as a coherent unity, with internal flowing into external mind and body. That is the reason man chooses his eternal home while here on earth.

In explaining the states in which man cannot be reformed because his external man is not free, *Divine Providence* 129-153 present several interesting examples. Serious disease does not change man's internal will, and in that sense the internal will remains free, inviolate. Yet reformation is not then possible, "because the reason is not then in a free state, for the state of the mind [*mens*] depends upon the state of the body. When the body is sick the mind also is sick, because of its separation from the world—if for no other reason."[145] Temporarily man's free will in spiritual things is suspended or impeded, because his internal will is not free to change. It is free from being changed from without, but neither can it bring about change from within until health is restored to external mind and body. (It should be noted, however, that if a person was already reformed, then he may be strengthened during sickness.)

Disease is seldom an example of one man's decisions affecting another's freedom. But the Writings show that the same principles apply in such man-produced afflictions as threats, punishments, and compelled worship.[146]

> Worship that is forced is corporeal, lifeless, vague and gloomy; corporeal because it is of the body and not of the mind, lifeless because there is no life in it, vague because there is no understanding in it, and gloomy because there is no heavenly delight in it. On the other hand, worship that is not forced, when it is genuine, is spiritual, living, clear and joyful: spiritual because there is spirit from the Lord in it, living because there is life from the Lord in it, clear because there is wisdom from the Lord in it, and joyful because there is heaven from the Lord in it.[147]

It has been suggested that the Lord simply does not permit wrongful compulsion of man by man. This may seem to be a comforting thought, but then why do the Writings warn against it?[148] How can compelled worship in fact be "harmful"[149] if it is never permitted? If compulsion did not restrict free choice, then there would be nothing wrong with priests compelling. The prohibition against compulsion in many passages implies that compulsion is possible and can have some real effect on others.

Moreover, the Writings give examples of compulsion that actually occur. While some people do not permit themselves to be compelled to religion, there are some people who do.[150] The following also make plain that sometimes man does harmfully compel man:

> He who is compelled to think what is true and do what is good is not reformed, but thinks falsity and wills evil all the more. All compulsion has this effect, as we may see from the records and examples of life....[151]
>
> No good ever comes from compulsion, as when a man is compelled by another man to do what is good....[152]
>
> A state of compulsion is ... in a word, every state of fear which takes away the use of sound reason. When an evil man who in a state of compulsion promises repentance and also does what is good, comes into a state of freedom, he returns into his former life of evil.[153]
>
> To compel a man is not to insinuate into his will, because it is then the will of another from which he acts; and therefore when he returns to his own will, that is, to his own freedom, this is rooted out.[154]
>
> That which is inseminated in Freedom remains, because it is inrooted in the very will of man, which is the being of his life. But that which is insinuated under compulsion does not remain,

> because what is of compulsion is not from the will of the man, but is from the will of him who compels. For this reason worship from freedom is pleasing to the Lord, but not worship from compulsion . . . .[155]
>
> Whatever is not rooted in freedom is dissipated on the first approach of evil and temptation.[156]
>
> [Some] are desirous that the things of faith should be believed in simplicity, without any mental view of them on the part of the rational, not being aware that not anything of faith, not even its deepest secret, is comprehended by any man without some rational idea, and also a natural one . . . . Hereby they may indeed protect themselves against those who reason about everything from what is negative . . . ; but to those who are in the affirmative concerning the Word . . . *such a position is hurtful, as they may thus take away from anyone his freedom of thought, and even bind the conscience to that which is in the highest degree heretical by in this way dominating both the internal and the external things of a man.*[157]

A number of passages, then, indicate that man's exercise of free will may be hindered or limited to some extent by the free actions of other men. We are reminded of the teachings noted earlier that man's freedom is in its perfection in his soul. Here it is inviolate. But as it descends into his lower planes it can be stopped, and freedom to be reformed may be hindered or temporarily suspended. (See THE ORGANIC UNITY OF MAN above.)

The possibility of harming others' freedom in spiritual things is the reason that in the spiritual sense of the Ten Commandments we are forbidden "to rob others of truths of their faith; and this is done by means of falsities and heresies. Priests [may be] spiritual thieves; for they rob the people of the means of salvation, which are the truths of faith."[159] "In *the spiritual sense* to bear false witness means to persuade people that what is false in faith is true, and that the evil of life is the good of life, and the reverse; but to do this purposely, and not from ignorance . . . ."[160] "*In the spiritual sense,* murder means every method of killing and destroying the souls of men. Varied and manifold are the methods employed, such as turning men away from God, religion and Divine worship, raising scandal against these, and persuasively insinuating aversion and loathing. Such murderers are all the devils and satans in hell . . . ."[161] Such prohibitions certainly imply that man can harm another's spiritual life and freedom to be reformed.[162]

An important passage in this connection is *Arcana Coelestia* 4171, which teaches that "actual evil" in man has "various origins—in general two: one, that he receives evil from others *through no fault* of his own; and the other, that he receives it of his own accord, thus through his own fault. That which a man receives from others without any fault of his own is what is signified in the Word by 'what is torn'. . . ." One example of this is a good man who is persuaded that not a life of good, but faith alone brings about salvation. If such a man "then becomes careless in regard to life, and even treats it with contempt, he is said to be 'torn'; for 'torn' is predicated of good into which falsity is insinuated, and *thereby* the good becomes no longer living." Another instance is of married partners who come into evil because they allow themselves to be persuaded that marriage is only for the sake of various worldly uses—"the result being that after he has received the persuasion the individual has no heavenly idea of marriage; and supposing that lasciviousness is the consequence, there then comes into existence that which is called 'torn'; and so in all other cases." Since such a person "receives evil from others without any fault of his own," eventually he is able to see the truth, live by it, and so be saved.[163] But it also would seem that the evil he has come into because of others will have some permanent consequences for him. While in another time and place he might have been hearing the truth and shunning evils so as to be led more directly through regeneration, instead his good becomes "no longer living", at least temporarily, and actual evils are brought into his life.

VIII
Divine Fairness and Human Equality

The doctrine that all can be regenerated, "every-one according to his state,"[164] can bear careful reflection. And we should be cautious with the teaching that those who are good but ignorant of Divine truth can be regenerated after death.[165] These doctrines do not say that whatever society man is born into, whatever heredity is passed on to him, whatever intellectual and affectional influences others exert on him, he can be reformed and regenerated in the same way as any other man. Those who are within the Lord's Church can be conjoined with the Lord "in respect to His Divine rational", but those who are without the Church, if they are good, "are conjoined with the Lord in respect to His Divine natural. They who have a still grosser kind [of holiness] are conjoined with the Lord in respect to His Divine sensual.... In this conjunction are those among the Gentiles who worship idols, and yet live in charity in accordance with their religion."[166] Thus the kind and level of conjunction with God that a person enjoys may depend partly on the type of church and society in which he lives.

Why should this be so? Man's spiritual development depends not only upon his free *will,* but also upon the *ideas* that are available to him for directing his thought and life. In explaining spiritual enlightenment, reformation and regeneration, *de Verbo* XII says that first the memory must have knowledges

> of spiritual and natural things, for these are the stores into which the Lord operates by means of the light of heaven, and the fuller these are and the more free from confirmed falsities, the more enlightened is the perception given and the clearer the conclusion. For the Divine operation does not fall into a man who is empty and void, as for example one who does not know that the Lord is pure love and pure mercy . . . ; or who does not know that the Word in the sense of the letter is written in many places from appearances. Such a man cannot be enlightened by the Word where it is said of Jehovah that He is wrathful and angry . . . .[167]

The truths that man does or does not come into contact with are of considerable importance to his regeneration or lack thereof. "To believe what is false is hurtful."[168] Else why would it matter whether man has contact with the Word? Though the Lord wills that every man be reborn to the celestial degree,[169] it is not said that all men born into the world have the same opportunities of celestial regeneration.

The ideology of democracy has many uses on the civil plane, but in considering spiritual things we must distinguish secular notions of equality from Divine ideas of equality. Every man can be regenerated, "according to his state," but such passages as the following show that the spiritual equality, fairness and justice do not imply spiritual sameness.

> Now since a man, a Christian, knows the Lord and has the Word, and since the Church is with him from the Lord by the Word, it is evident that he *more than a man not a Christian* has the ability to become regenerated and so to become spiritual, and also to attain love truly conjugial.... After death the damnation of Christian polygamists is more severe than the damnation of those who commit only natural adultery.[170]

> *For the Israelitish nation it was permitted to marry more wives than one because with that nation there was no Christian Church, and hence no possibility of love truly conjugial....* They with whom the Christian Church does not exist are natural men, both internally and externally. With such men polygamy, being inscribed on the natural man, is not hurtful; for, as regards love in marriage, the natural man perceives only such things as belong to lust. The Lord... alone opens the internal things of human minds and, making them spiritual, implants them in things

natural, that these also may receive a spiritual essence. This they do receive if man approaches Him and lives according to His precepts.[171]

It is permitted Mohammedans at this day to marry many wives because they do not acknowledge the Lord Jesus Christ to be one with the Father, and thus as the God of heaven and earth, and hence cannot receive love truly conjugial . . . . The followers of Mohammed could not acknowledge our Lord as any God from eternity, but only as a perfect natural man . . . . They could not but pass the Lord by . . . . They do not know what the Lord taught. It is from this cause that the interiors of their mind . . . could not be opened; that they can be opened only by the Lord, see no. 340 just above. The genuine reason why they are opened by the Lord when He is acknowledged and is approached as the God of heaven and earth is because otherwise there is no conjunction, and without conjunction there is no reception.[172]

[Polygamists] remain natural and do not become spiritual; and the natural man cannot see that there is any sin in such things as are of the received religion; this the spiritual man alone sees.[173]

Although they may have heard and read these things, yet they cannot give up the idea which was conceived in boyhood and *confirmed in them afterwards*

> *by their teachers, and which has so closed up their rational faculty that they are incapable of seeing, that is, of understanding these words of the Lord....* [174]

> The men of the Ancient Church, and still more the men of the Israelitish Church, were external and natural men, *nor could they become internal and spiritual,* as men can since the Lord's coming.[175]

The time and place of man's life, and the quality of truths with which he comes into contact, would seem to have considerable influence on his freedom and ability to be regenerated.[176]

Some have argued that such passages refer only to regeneration on earth, and that all such apparent inequities are rectified by the possibility of regeneration after death.[177] Can non-Christians be regenerated later, and polygamists eventually receive love truly conjugial? In fact something of this does take place, but apparently only to a limited degree. Some Moslems, for example, become Christians after death and receive genuine conjugial love. But others do not, and there is a distinctly Moslem heaven of two planes. It is outside the Christian heaven, and while in the higher Moslem heaven they live with one wife only and acknowledge the Lord Jesus Christ as *equal with* God the Father, in the lower Moslem heaven they live in polygamy, "honorably."[178] In neither heaven is the Lord Jesus Christ acknowledged as *one* with God the Father.[179] Thus living a Moslem life does not necessarily deprive a person of receiving Christianity and conjugial love. But the two-fold Moslem heaven demonstrates that with many the Moslem religion exerts a strong influence and limits their ability and freedom to become Christian.

Thus the ability to be regenerated (referred to in CL 339-341, 348)—an ability limited by the quality of truths which a man is taught—does not refer merely to regeneration on earth. The persistence of the lowest heavens shows that limited spiritual development on earth leads many to a relatively low state of heavenly good as their *eternal* lot. The quality of truth which a church and society come to value through the generations has major consequences in determining the eternal spiritual home of those who are nurtured therein. It is difficult to believe, for example, that the free decisions of many generations who established Moslem life and values have not influenced and limited the freedom of their Moslem descendants; that regardless of the free decisions of those past generations, the Moslem heavens would exist anyway. If some Moslems today live in polygamy in a low natural heaven, must not that fact result partly from the free decisions of previous generations to live in polygamy? The very reason a good Moslem can be polygamous in his heaven is because of polygamy in the religion in which he was raised. The Lord has permitted Islam so to teach for very good reasons,[180] but polygamy was not from Him; it could only have come from the ways of life chosen by many past generations of men.

When we read that "everyone is reformed according to his state and faculty,"[181] we should take care to emphasize "according to his state and faculty." The parable of the talents[182] teaches a variety in individual spiritual capabilities. "All who are being reformed and regenerated are gifted with charity and faith by the Lord, but each according to his faculty and his state; for there are evils and falsities with which man has imbued himself from infancy, which stand in the way of one person's receiving a like gift with another .... [Remains] are acquired from infancy even to the time of reformation, with one person more, with another fewer."[183] Can it be the Lord's doing if one has received more remains than another? Apparently human decisions—in this case, especially parents'—can affect the quality of another's eternal life, for "according to the quality and quantity of the remains—that is, of the good and truth with a man—does he enjoy bliss and happiness in the other life ...."[184]

"Unfair!" cries out the democracy in which we

have been educated, and with which our concepts are permeated. But "My thoughts are not your thoughts, neither are your ways My ways, saith the Lord. For as the heavens are higher than the earth, so are My ways higher than your ways, and My thoughts than your thoughts."[185] The only way to understand true fairness is not to extrapolate from human documents (however enlightened on the civil plane), but to learn from Divine revelation what Divine fairness actually is. Before we insist that Providence would not allow something, let us see from the Word just what Providence does and does not permit. When we think some Divine way is unfair, we may simply not yet understand what Divine justice is.

Divine fairness in fact exceeds human fairness because the Lord treats everyone not as the same, but as the unique individual he is. Human equality tends towards sameness, but the Divine accommodates to each individual in a manner unique to that individual. We should be more impressed with the Lord's ability to accommodate to every human state and to save people surrounded from birth to death by gross falsities and disorders, than we should be disturbed by the apparent inequity arising from His inability to change men after death and make them all true Christians.

Divine Providence 254 in particular speaks to this point:

> For it makes no difference whether they are in such joy as that experienced by the angels of the highest heaven or by the angels of the lowest heaven, since everyone who enters heaven comes into the highest joy of his own heart; anything greater he does not assume, for he would be suffocated by it. For illustration of this compare a peasant and a king. A peasant may be in a state of the highest joy when he goes about in a new suit of rough homespun, and sits down at a table on which is pork, a piece of beef, cheese, beer and common wine; and he would be distressed at heart if he were to be clothed like a king in purple, silk, gold and silver, and if a table were to be set for him with delicacies and costly food of many kinds with noble wine. From this it is clear that there is heavenly happiness for the last as well as for the first, for each in his degree . . . .[186]

If both a thimble and a bucket are filled, it cannot be said that one is more full than the other; each is filled to capacity.

Dissatisfaction at apparent inequalities of heavenly blessing would appear to involve a desire by the natural man for more of a heavenly reward than would be suitable or even bearable for a given human life. But "in heavenly joy there is never anything connected with being pre-eminent to others, and . . . in proportion as there is this, there is hell."[187] Surely the lower angels do not find themselves dissatisfied because higher angels have "more" joy than they. Envy simply has no place in heaven.[188] To the natural man the desire for heavenly equality seems only fair, but Divine revelation testifies that the natural man does not appreciate the ways of God.

But would we really want it any other way? Would we really want Providence so to control human relationships that whatever we say and do to another, there would never be any lasting effects on him? Do we really want our free choices to affect only ourselves in a permanent way? Would we be happy believing that however we decide to act towards others, the Lord will ensure that only the utmost good will ever result? How would we like to believe that our every word and deed will make no real difference to anyone else, will matter not a whit except to ourselves? What may seem fair to the natural man would in fact enclose every human in a tight little box from which he could have no genuine relationship with anyone, except with God and with self. Every human relationship is in fact illusion, unless by our free choices we can have real and lasting influences on others.

It appears, then, that not only is man free in some degree in his natural actions, but he may also, through his decisions, have important and even eternal influences, good or evil, upon others—

influences that would otherwise not take place. One man's free decisions may even restrict or temporarily suspend another's freedom and rationality. Further study is needed to examine *how great* an eternal effect one may have upon another. *How much* will various states of non-freedom or restricted freedom affect a man's eternal life?[189] How great is the influence of past generations' free decisions upon a present generation's eternal free choices? How responsible is man for another's eternal happiness?[190] Parent for child? Spouse for spouse?

The unanswered questions are many, and we may never attain precise answers in day-to-day life.[191] My present concern is simply to establish that some such lasting influences exist. Were this not so, the study of human relationships would have no spiritual relevance.

The applications to life are myriad. For example, organized New Church bodies have generally stood strongly for the protection of the freedom of individuals associated in any way with the Church. This would be irrelevant if the Lord by Himself alone protected man's free will in spiritual things. If freedom of speech and action were not important for preserving man's freedom in spiritual things, there would be no serious reason for preserving freedom of speech and action. New Church leaders have written eloquently to show that free speech and action are essential to the life of the Church.[192] The political and social implications are likewise far reaching.

Man's freedom, then, is not purely spiritual and unconnected with actual life on earth. Because man is an organic unity, his spiritual life and freedom are connected with what he actually does, with what goes on around him, and with truth available to him. The spiritual and natural are created to be one in man and his spiritual freedom is related to his natural freedom as fountain to stream,[193] even as his love and action are closely connected by correspondences. It is because all things in man are connected that human beings should co-operate with the Lord to respect and protect each other's freedom.

IX
How the Lord Governs Evil

If the Lord does not determine (cause) all things that happen in the natural world, the question arises, how does He govern evil and restrain it? One way He does not govern it is by simply never letting evil happen. What He permits is still evil. Permission of evil is only for the sake of good, but this does not mean that only good is permitted. Part of the Lord's governing of evil is allowing it to happen.

The question of *how* the Lord governs evil is one of the most difficult in theology, because good and evil are opposites and repel each other. Would not the Lord's governing presence with evil men torment and destroy their life? Their every effort is to flee from His good and truth. Yet we are taught frequently that the Lord's Providence is in every least singular, and somehow the Divine does govern evil men and the evils they do. "The Divine Providence, not only with the good but also with the evil, is universal in the veriest singulars; and yet it is not in men's evils."[194]

"And yet it is not in men's evils." Of course it could not be in their evils, and perhaps this is the key to seeing how the Lord governs evil. He cannot be with evil men in their hearts because this would only torture them. Rather His Divine truth can be present with them through some degree of enforced order in the externals of life. Thus the Lord is present in the hells and rules them by the external restraints of punishment and fear of punishment. "It ought to be known that the sole means of restraining the violence and fury of those who are in the hells is the fear of punishment. There is no other way."[195] Particularly malicious devils are set over the hells as governors, and sometimes angels look into the hells and moderate their insanities and disturbances.[196] The methods of governing hell are external, since the Lord cannot bring the devils' wills into order.

In the world punishments and the fears thereof are not the only means of governing evil. There are fears also for reputation, honor and gain, which depend to some extent upon the external customs and traditions in society. There are also laws and formal civil punishments on earth. The Writings say a great deal about the use of these means, but the method is always external—to keep the worst evils from destroying society and the human race. The evil "are led by the Lord but only by means of external bonds, which are fears on account of the penalties of the law and loss of reputation, honor, gain, and consequently pleasures. He leads them also by means of worldly rewards."[197]

But the Lord also operates interiorly into the evil—not into their evil hearts, but into their unpervertable inmost souls. This inflowing operation does not stop their evils, but it does so regulate them that they may be continually restored to equilibrium and freedom, and so that some use may be served by their evils. One of the most comforting passages in the Writings says that the Lord's Providence

> ... continually grants permission for the sake of the end, and permits such things as belong to the end *and no others;* and the evils that proceed by permission it continually keeps under view, separates and purifies, *sending away and removing by unknown ways whatever is not consistent with the end* [which is salvation]. These things are brought about in man's interior will, and from this in his interior thought.[198]

"Nothing is permitted except for the end that some good may come out of it ...."[199] "In the universal spiritual world reigns the end which proceeds from the Lord, which is that nothing whatever, not even the least thing, shall arise, except that good may come from it."[200] When some evil occurs, it is useful to search out the good that sooner or later results from it. Appreciating this good should make the permission somewhat understandable, and demonstrate that the evil was not in fact the unmitigated tragedy that at first it may have appeared to be.

This comforting doctrine does not mean, however, that evil that is permitted is basically a good. Though good come out of it, evil is still evil. Good resulting from evil may not negate the evil, even though it moderates and mitigates it to some extent. This is obvious from the fact that some people choose to go to hell. Thus *Arcana Coelestia* 6489, just quoted above, continues:

> But as man has freedom, in order that he may be reformed, he is bent from evil to good so far as he allows himself to be bent in freedom, and (if he cannot be led to heaven) continually from the most atrocious hell, into which he makes every effort to plunge, into a milder one.

Much evil that is permitted results in eternal damnation, but still the Lord has kept the man free, and He has regulated the evil so that milder forms of evil and pain result than man would have chosen if left to himself.[201]

The Lord's secret inner regulation of man is not by itself sufficient to restrain evil, because external restraints are also said to be necessary. Interior regulation of man's states keeps the evil man in equilibrium and freedom,[202] but the Writings put considerable emphasis upon the regulation of evils by external restraints. "The will and understanding of men function under this free choice; but the commission of evil in both worlds, the spiritual and the natural, is restrained by laws; otherwise society in both worlds would perish."[203] The commentary on this heading states that this truth is so evident that it does not require explanation. "Without external restraints" not only would society perish, but also the entire human race, because man is obsessed by the loves of self and the world.[204]

We should see what this important teaching says and what it does not say. It does not say that man has no freedom in natural actions. It implies rather that he has some such freedom, since if he did not, then external restraints would not be needed. They are needed because he is given freedom in action. The teaching does say that this freedom of action is and should be restrained by external means, to some degree at least.[205] Yet evil in action is still possible. In hell it is a daily occurrence, in spite of restraints. That evil in action occurs also in this world despite restraints, is not only evident to common perception but is also taught in the passage just referred to:

> That such is the inner nature of man becomes evident in seditious tumults, when the restraints of law are thrown off; and also in the slaughter

> and pillage which ensue when the signal is given to the victors to vent their fury on besieged townspeople who have been vanquished; scarcely one stays his hand till the order is heard. It is clear, therefore, that if men were not restrained by fear of punishment inflicted by law, not only society but also the whole human race would be destroyed.[206]

Man's evils do sometimes break out. "When evil enters the will, then it does harm, for then it also goes forth into act whenever external bonds do not restrain."[207]

In general the Lord rules the evil by an outermost plane of apparent conscience, which is really a sort of enlightened self-interest; "without this government these [the evil] would rush into all wicked and insane things, and do so rush when they are without the restraints of this plane. All those who do not allow themselves to be ruled by means of these planes are either insane, or punished according to the laws."[208] Evil can actually be *removed* only by the "true use of free will in spiritual things,"[209] and when through misuse of free will evil is active, then the means of control are external—punishments and fears. When these external means for some reason fail, as in war and revolution, hell literally breaks loose. History, sadly, is abundant in examples. This is not a comforting realization when we observe the failure of society's customary external restraints and fears, but we should not evade the truth because of its discomfort.

There are other means also by which the Lord governs evil. Often selfish motivation is used for unintended good purposes, "The Lord provides for His ends through the evil equally as through the good; for the Lord moves the evil through their very loves to do what is good to the neighbor, to their country, and the church.... In order that they may perform such things as are conducive to the public good, successes are also given them in accordance with their projects, which successes are greater incitements to them from the fact that they ascribe them to themselves."[210] Good external achievements often result from the loves of self and the world.[211]

No one studies history for long without realizing how frequently events intended by man for one purpose bring about something entirely different. Many historical movements, such as the French Revolution as it actually developed, resulted from no conscious intention by anyone. No one planned the Renaissance or the decline and fall of the Roman Empire. Paul's egotism was used for the establishment of the first Christian Church. The Israelites were used as a representative of a church to maintain communication between the Divine and the human race; they thought they were a chosen people for reasons almost opposite to the truth. Pagan, idolatrous tribes were used to punish the Israelites, and wars that take place today serve similar hidden uses.[212] It appears that pagan Rome's love of dominion and external order was used so that the first Christian Church could grow. Impatient Henry VIII's longing for a male heir (along with some fascinating contemporary political and military relationships) served for the establishment of religious freedom in England and so among English-speaking peoples. Worldly loves of conquest, gold and glory were used to spread the Word throughout the world.[213] History and a man's own life are replete with examples of self-serving loves bringing about unintended good consequences.

It is also possible that the Lord uses the time of man's death in order to govern evil.[214] This is speculation, however, and some students of the Writings believe rather that the time of death is not determined by the Lord, but only foreseen by Him; and that from this foresight the Lord prepares man for his death. The role of the time of man's death in the government of evil needs further study.

Even more is further study needed on the subject of natural disasters—not those misfortunes which are the work of man, and which are therefore permissions, but physical disasters that happen apparently without human cause, such as earthquakes, volcanos, floods, serious storms, fires started by lightning. Are these in fact "acts of God," as insurance companies suggest? They are often closely connected with important historical events, not to mention death and suffering.

The weather plays a crucial role in history—particularly in its effect on military affairs and on the harvest, since hungry people frequently do things they would not otherwise do. Unusual growth of the fungus ergot on rye in France in 1789 was a major factor contributing to the mass delusion known as the "Great Fear," which in turn helped precipitate the French Revolution. The "Protestant Wind" in 1588 (which played an enormous part in destroying the Spanish fleet and so preserving religious freedom in England) was most unusual at that season. Did Divine Providence bring about the unusual winds for the sake of religious liberty, or foresee that the wind and storms would be there, and insinuate into the Spanish commanders when and where they should sail?[215] Or did Providence do none of these, or something else?

Some other historical examples include the destruction of ancient Cretan civilization by an apparent earthquake and tidal wave; an eclipse during the Athenian invasion of Sicily which led to major developments in the Peloponnesian War, on account of the Greeks' superstition; the terrible earthquake in Lisbon in 1756; the destruction of Sodom and Gomorrah; the cyclones that periodically ravage peoples who live near oceans; the winter of 1941-1942 in Russia; and the weather and tidal conditions in the English Channel in 1940, and again in June, 1944.

Different students of the Writings see such events in different ways. Some believe the Lord directly controls natural ultimates like the weather and other purely physical forces. The basis for this interpretation lies in the doctrines of Providence operating in every least singular, and of government of mediates by means of ultimates.[216] Consider also such passages as the following: "There is no such thing as chance, and . . . apparent accident or fortune, is Providence in the ultimate of order . . . ."[217] "The truth Divine which flows into the third heaven nearest the Lord, also at the same time and without successive formation flows in down to the ultimates of order, and there from the First immediately also rules and provides each and all things . . . ."[218] The weather in the land of Canaan before the Lord's First Coming appears to have varied at least somewhat according to the spiritual states of the Israelites.[219]

Other students doubt that the Lord intervenes in the natural operation of the weather in any special way. They suggest rather that the Lord foresees purely natural events that occur in the fixed ultimate patterns of this world (produced by "non-living endeavors") and uses them by preparing men for their consequences and by secretly guiding men to be present or absent during their occurrence.[220]

The subject remains an open question. When a disastrous earthquake, storm or drought takes place, what are its causes—fixed, unchanging patterns in nature, or an immediate influx into physical ultimates that causes some unusual natural event? To what extent is nature alive? What is meant by non-living endeavor?[221] How does spiritual influx into dead elementary matter differ from influx into man, animal, and plant? Perhaps the alternatives are not very far apart, but further study is needed.

The foregoing surveys some of the general teachings about how the Lord governs the doing of evil. The universal to hold in mind is that no evil is permitted except for the sake of some good end. The Writings invite us to see these goods,[222] but we should not think that such goods will always negate the evils. Man may resist every effort of the Lord and do his best to precipitate himself into evil and slavery. It may even be possible for man to live in such a way that he destroys his own freedom of choice.[223] Morever, though permission results in some good, the evil that is permitted remains evil and is not a good. The Lord's permitting is good because He can do only good, but what He permits is evil, and, if man would allow, something better would be preferable. The degeneration of men before the Lord's First Coming was a permisssion, beautifully governed by the Lord so that the individual was still free to be saved, and so that even worse evils were avoided, until the Lord by His Coming could bring redemption. But this degeneration was still evil, not willed by God, but chosen by man.

It is an important question because if we try too hard to see universal human existence as good, we may come to see what is evil as good. Some even have come to feel that whatever they choose to do, the Lord will protect and care for them. Though in practical application the distinction between good and evil often seems fuzzy, spiritually the difference between them is the difference between heaven and hell.[224] The need to see good in others should not make us so fearful of intolerance that we refuse to recognize disorder or to believe in the existence of evil.[225] Everyone wants to understand good, but it is his understanding of evil and ability to distinguish it from good that will set man's course, on earth and after death.

X
Providence and Order

In order to understand how the Lord governs the human race we must see more than the ends, uses, and goods of Providence. We must study also the means, truths, and order of Providence—even as any use is defined by the order associated with it, or any good by its truth. To know what the Lord *wishes* is not enough. We must also understand *what means* He uses.

The first and universal law of the order of Providence—repeated frequently in the Writings—is that man is a free and rational being, and can be changed only by means of that freedom and rationality. The direction of man's life is to a large extent his to determine, not because he always does a good job at it, but because otherwise man would not be man. This is expressed clearly in *Arcana Coelestia* 6487:

> When I was talking with the angels about the Divine Providence of the Lord, there were spirits also present, who had impressed on themselves some notion about fate or absolute necessity. *They supposed the Lord to act from necessity,* because He cannot

> proceed otherwise than according to the things that belong to the most perfect order. But they were shown that man has freedom, and that *if he acts from freedom, it is not from necessity.* This was illustrated by the case of houses which are to be built, in that the bricks, mortar, sand, stones serving for foundations and columns, also timbers and beams, and the like, are brought together not in that order in which the house is to be constructed, but at pleasure; and that the Lord alone knows what kind of house *may* be built with these materials. All the things which are from the Lord are most essential; but *they do not follow in order from necessity, but in a manner that is applicable to the freedom of man.*[226]

Where man acts from freedom, it is not from necessity. Why is this central to the order of Providence? Otherwise man would not be man and could have no life or happiness, not even the fleeting pleasures of hell. This would frustrate the Divine love, which above all wishes that others may have life as if their own.[227]

In a series of lectures delivered at Cambridge in 1948 Professor Herbert Butterfield spoke of Providence in history in a manner reminiscent of the passage just quoted.

> We might say that this human story is like a piece of orchestral music that we are playing over for the first time. In our presumption we may act as though we were the composer of the piece or try to bring out our own particular part as the

leading one. But in reality I personally only see the part of, shall we say, the second clarinet, and of course even within the limits of that I never know what is coming after the page that now lies open before me. None of us can have already played it over together, and even so the meaning of a passage may not be clear all at once—just as the events of 1914 only begin to be seen in perspective in the 1940's. If I am sure that B flat is the next note that I have to play I can never feel certain that it will not come with surprising implications until I have heard what the other people are going to play at the same moment. And no single person in the orchestra can have any idea when or where this piece of music is going to end.

Even this analogy is not sufficiently flexible to do justice to the processes of time; and to make the comparison more authentic we must imagine that the composer himself is only composing the music inch by inch as the orchestra is playing it; so that if you and I play wrong notes he changes his mind and gives a different turn to the bars that come immediately afterwards, as though saying to himself: 'We can only straighten out this piece of untidiness if we pass for a moment from the major into the minor key.' Indeed the composer of the piece leaves himself room for great elasticity, until we ourselves have shown what we are going to do next; although when the music has actually been played over and has become a thing of the past we may be tempted to imagine that it is just as he had

> intended it to be all the time—that the whole course of things had been inevitable from the first. If we were helping a small boy to ride a bicycle on an indefinite stretch of sand, we should not feel that each time he swerved and then tried to right himself we had to rectify his aberrations by bringing the course back into something like the straight line on which we had started the ride. We should be prepared for a considerable elasticity in regard to the general drift and direction of the whole expedition. In fact we should be playing Providence over a free creature; though I have no doubt that the particles in the fabric of the bicycle would be able to prove that the machine was guiding itself.[228]

Except for the suggestion that the composer changes his mind if you and I play wrong notes, this passage appears to present an accurate description of how history develops. The Writings show that God, far from changing his mind, foresees what all men will do, and provides or "composes" accordingly.[229]

The Lord could not grant man merely an inner spiritual freedom and then determine everything else without depriving man of the freedom to enjoy life as of himself. Freedom in natural events as well as spiritual is just one of many gifts that the Lord grants in addition to freedom of will and understanding. Let us look at some of the other things the Lord gives us for the sake of human life and happiness, in addition to freedom in actions:

1) Hereditary tendencies to good and evil.
2) Continued life among men on earth, even if free will is abused.
3) Spiritual spheres emanating from the character of man and spirit.
4) An order of influx and communication from spirit to spirit, and from the spiritual world into men in the natural world.
5) Influx of good and evil into natural forms on earth, producing both good uses and evil uses.[230]
6) An eternal character in accordance with our use of free will in spiritual things.
7) An ability to be ourselves after death, fully in the heavens, and in a more limited way in the hells.
8) Eternal association with others of similar character to our own.
9) A spiritual environment in correspondence with our eternal character.
10) An ability to make fantasies according to our eternal character, if we so wish.
11) Historical development in the spiritual world (a sequence not of time, but of succession of states) involving false heavens, imprisonment and infestation of simple good spirits in the lower earth, various other disorders, and three cataclysmic spiritual judgments.

Surely this list could be greatly expanded.

Now all these provisions and allowances, though intended to enrich human life, are frequently abused and corrupted by man. Yet they are given us because without them man could not enjoy the life that the Lord wishes to give us. What would life be like without any of these? The Lord truly loves us and gives us so much for our happiness, even though he knows we may choose to abuse every gift. He gives all these because He loves us and wants us to be happy.

The gift of free will in natural actions is thus but one of many things the Lord grants in addition to the purely spiritual freedom of affection and thought. As human life would suffer without any of the gifts listed above, so also would it suffer if there were no freedom in natural action. The reasons involve primarily the organic unity of man, or of his will and thought with his action and speech. The following passage sums up the necessity of some freedom in action:

> The reason why the evil succeed in accordance with their skill, is that it is according to order that everyone should do what he does from reason and also from freedom; and therefore unless it were left to man to act in freedom according to his reason, and thus also unless the consequent arts succeeded, the man could not possibly be disposed to receive eternal life.... Unless a man is kept in the freedom to do evil also, good from the Lord cannot be provided for him.[231]

Doing and succeeding are part of life even as are willing and thinking. This is why man's freedom to do is of order.

The order of Providence is not difficult to understand abstractly, but holding it in mind in practical applications is another matter. "It is one thing to think from causes, and another to think about causes . . . ."[232] Similarly it is one thing to know the order of Providence, and another to think from it. It is one thing to know the doctrine of free will, and another to think from it.

I submit that the doctrines of Providence and free will are difficult to enter into sufficiently so as to think from them. The appearance to the natural man is that Providence operates sporadically, in special acts that go beyond or against the normal order of things; and that man is a non-free machine that is caused to do things, rather than something that is free in itself. The truth is that Providence is always operating, always according to order, present both in apparent fortune and misfortune. And man cannot be said to be *caused to do whatever he does freely.*[233] When man is free, *nothing* causes or makes him do something—nothing except his own free decision. Yet it is difficult to think in this way; modern man searches for the causes of all things, including human feelings, ideas, and decisions. Many social scientists believe that the causes of everything human gradually will become known. Surely there is much to learn about causes in human actions, relationships, and development. Yet when we study man we reach a point where we cannot know if he did something on account of some cause outside of himself, or because he freely, arbitrarily decided in himself that he was going to do it. To the extent that the latter is the case, the scientific study of man is limited and must yield to the theological truth that man is endowed by his Maker with freedom.

Reflection upon *True Christian Religion* 502 suggests the difficulty we have in thinking *from* the order of Providence. This passage lists many questions which man will ask if he does not understand that Divine omnipotence operates according to order:

> He would, therefore, ask such absurd quesions as these: "Why did the Lord come into the world, and in this way bring about redemption when God, by His omnipotence, could have accomplished the same work from heaven as He brought about when on earth? Why should He not, by redemption, have saved the whole human race without exception, and why should the devil afterwards be able to prevail over the Redeemer in man? Why is there a hell? Could not God, from His omnipotence, have blotted it out, and can He not now blot it out, or deliver all from it and make them angels of heaven? Why a last judgment? Could not God transfer all the goats from the left hand to the

> right, and make them sheep? . . . Why did He not originally, or why does He not still, make the whole world a paradise, where there should be no tree of knowledge of good and evil, and no serpent? where all the hills should flow with generous wines, and yield gold and silver each in its virgin state? and where all men might live as images of God with songs of jubilee, and with perpetual festivity and rejoicing? Would not all this be worthy of an omnipotent God?" These and similar questions would he ask.
>
> But, my friend, this is all idle talk. The Divine omnipotence is not without order. God Himself is Order; and from order, in order and for order. There is an order into which man was created, namely, that his happiness or his misery should depend on his free will in spiritual things. For, as was said above, without free will man could not have been created.

They are all absurd questions, but the frequency with which they (or their modern variations) are asked suggests that the order of Providence is easier to think *about* than to think *from.* To know about the order of Providence and free will is not to *think from* that order.

Faced with opposition to their will, men throughout history have attacked the concept of free will and have sought to force on others their own brand of goodness. A perennial popular idea is that the evil do not stay in hell to eternity—which is really a denial of man's free choice in spiritual things.[234] Much legislative reform, particularly on social issues, tries to provide answers to problems that can really be solved only by change of the human heart through free will. Today's intellectual climate of opinion contains much that is negative towards free will, and affirmative instead towards conditioning and compelling man, as an animal or a machine, into various human concepts of good. The Lord guards man's freedom as man guards the pupil of his eye,[235] but when man finds his will frustrated, the principle of freedom is often the first to be challenged.

One of the reasons New Church men may not think from this doctrine as fully as they might is perhaps that their freedom is in practice not seriously threatened. They generally try to respect the freedom of others and believe parents should not totally dominate their children. In spite of some gradual and subtle government encroachments, the New Church and its institutions have enjoyed considerable freedom of action and may not feel individual freedom under attack. It may be that serious struggle against threats to freedom is necessary for man to enter fully into the doctrine of Providence and free will. Historically, increased understanding of freedom, and respect for others' freedom, have emerged from periods of conflict; one example of this is the establishment of the

General Church of the New Jerusalem. It is no accident that some of the clearest statements concerning freedom have come from New Church leaders who daily wrestle with the question of preserving the freedom of the church while still providing for its uses. If in fact struggle is needed to understand Providence and freedom, the coming generations may provide that struggle.

XI
Some Difficulties

The view presented in this study has emphasized human freedom as cause of both spiritual decisions and natural events of good and evil. The question arises whether this interpretation contradicts the doctrine that man's own prudence is nothing, and that Divine Providence does everything good. In the book *Divine Providence* an entire chapter is given to the subject: "There is no such thing as man's own prudence. It only appears that there is, and there ought to be this appearance; but the Divine Providence is universal because it is in things most individual."[236] What is meant by man's own prudence being nothing?

Man's *own* prudence is defined as coming not from God, but from his *proprium*, or what is his own.[237] This kind of prudence is not really prudence at all, because wisdom, to be wise, must come from God rather than from self. In this sense man's "own" or "proprial" prudence is nothing, because the prudence of him who thinks he is wise from himself is in fact folly. But "proprial prudence" does exist, and indeed is the means by which evil and falsity, and thus hell, are appropriated to the man who believes in his own prudence rather than in Divine Providence. Similarly the Writings can say that evil "has no reality" in that it "has no power and no spiritual life,"[238] but it certainly does exist! "Evil, regarded in itself, is not nothing, although it is the nullity of good."[239] Proprial prudence is indeed a factor in human life, but it produces nothing good and has nothing to do with genuine prudence.

Divine Providence, not man's own prudence, is the source of everything good.[240] When man does good by means of a free choice of good, the essence of his choice is love which he receives from the Lord. It is the Lord's good, even though he chooses it. His own prudence did not lead him to it. The Divine led him to it, and good from the Divine inflowed so that he could choose well. Man cannot justly take credit for the reception of good and should ascribe to the Lord everything that may be good with him, because it was inflowing good that inspired the choice of good.[241] Thus Divine Providence does everything good, and man's own prudence does nothing of good, though it may appear to do good. If man's own prudence really does nothing at all and has no freedom to do evil, then we must ascribe evil to the Lord.

This does not suggest that man should slack his

hands and wait for the Divine Providence to do everything. Rather man should seek to be truly prudent, from God not from self. As *Divine Providence* sums up, "If, therefore, you wish to be led by the Divine Providence, use prudence as a servant and steward does who faithfully dispenses the goods of his master. This prudence is the talent which was given to the servants to trade with, of which they must render an account."[242] Genuine human prudence is something to be acquired and used in the service of the Lord. This true prudence is not proprial prudence, but man's free reception of the Divine Providence, and thus it is really Providence. Man is free to be led either by it or by his proprial prudence.

The teachings about man's own prudence do not call human freedom into question, but rather turn man to a living acknowledgment of the Lord as source of all truth and good. This does not denigrate the doctrine of human freedom and responsibility. Rather it redefines man's freedom as essentially a choice between trusting proprial prudence and accepting prudence from God. For when prudence is used as a wise servant would use it, it is Providence.

But perhaps all this doctrinal elaboration is fallacious. It can be argued that the appearance that we are free in our actions and free to affect others, is a necessary appearance, but not really true. Perhaps we are meant to *believe* we can, by our free actions, affect others, whereas in actual fact we cannot.[243] Man's life appears to be his own, but it is not really his own; that also is a necessary appearance, but not a true one. Might it also be a false but necessary appearance that we are free in our actions?

It must be admitted that this is possible, but there are substantial arguments against this interpretation. The appearance that all life is from self is indeed a necessary appearance, but investigation of the truth in this case does not destroy, but liberates and saves. Even while he feels life is his own, man is supposed to know and acknowledge the truth that all life is the Lord's. The celestial perceive this truth, and the more they acknowledge that good and truth and all life are the Lord's, the more they feel life to be their own. All life is the Lord's—the angels even *love* that this is so.[244] The Writings frequently invite and indeed command man to acknowledge this truth. Man is thus told to acknowledge that the appearance of self-life is not the truth, even though it is a necessary appearance.

And so it is with all appearances: we are invited to investigate and be freed by the truth. If there were an appearance that was supposed to remain, while the truth about it was supposed to continue hidden, then the problem arises that the truth is harmful to man, and that to believe in falsity is good. This seems to contradict everything that the Writings teach about good and truth. How can a false appearance be preferable to the truth? Truth is Divine. Truth is the means of approaching the Divine, and if we say we should believe in a falsity, and should not see the truth, then there would seem to be a serious obstacle between us and the Lord. Doubt would also be cast upon everything the Lord says: maybe many other teachings are simply appearances, untrue, and maybe the truth really is not good for man. Yet the universal teaching is that truth is the form of good. Man is supposed to understand the truth, or else his faith remains historical, natural and persuasive. Truth is the path to good. It is a fact that for certain ages, times and states, appearances are necessary.[245] But rational adults who can be regenerated by the Lord are invited again and again to see the truth and to put away fallacious appearances. The truth makes man free—genuinely free—by opening him to the freedom of heaven.[246]

This is why I cannot believe it is a false appearance in the Writings that we are free in our actions and free to affect others. If the appearance is false, then investigation of the truth in this case would not liberate and free, but imprison man in a pit of self-centered isolation. For example, let us suppose that every free decision we make will ultimately be for the best in others (because it is only an appearance that we are free to affect others, and in fact Providence does everything). Then our decisions matter only for ourselves. They appear to affect others, but this is fallacious. Does not this make the whole of religion and the life of charity and use self-centered? If all our decisions relating to other people have no effect on them, because everything is determined by Providence, then an enormous part of our lives seems to become meaningless, and the effect of seeing the truth is to turn us into ourselves. If we are responsible only for our own inner attitudes, then any time we consider a policy or action we are correct to reason, "It won't make any difference; the best will surely happen; the only thing that matters is that my own attitude be proper and good." Confronted with a disobedient child, father or mother should concentrate not on what is best for the child, since that does not make any difference to the child, but on his own motive only; whether he spanks, or reprimands, or lets the matter slide, does not matter. Only one's own motive matters.

Is it possible to live this way? Such a belief about the irrelevancy of what we do to others would seem to encourage us to be totally self-centered. Man cannot try to improve his motive without believing that his decisions have effects, and if he believes that nothing he does can affect others, how can he get out of himself? To correct his motive, man must think more about his neighbor's good than his own. But if what we do does not affect our neighbor, we cannot honestly direct our lives to the good of the neighbor. How can we plan good for him if we know our actions will not make us better vehicles for good? How can we shun evil against him if we know we can not really be harmful to him? We could shun evil *motive* as a sin against God and as harmful to ourselves, but not evil *action* because we would correctly say, "Nothing I do can really hurt him; I will concern myself only with my own inner feelings." But in order to correct our inner affections and motives we must also plan to do goods and shun evils so that the neighbor will be benefited as ourselves.[247] If we do not believe we can be of use to the neighbor through our decisions, we live in total isolation.

Thus if it is a fallacious appearance that we are free to affect others, it is an appearance that cannot endure investigation; the truth would destroy religion and charity and make man self-centered in any age, time or state, because man must live in the appearance that he can affect others. If this is a fallacious appearance, the consequence is that the truth is harmful to man under virtually all circumstances, and how can the truth be harmful to man? If any truth is such that it should never be investigated, it separates us from God in a most terrible way.

Something similar might be said to the suggestion that the whole subject is a Divine mystery: we cannot understand it, we never will, and it is useless to try. "I believe I am free, I feel free in natural things and free to affect others, but I also believe Providence does everything, and for the best." It is true that we cannot understand everything at once, and we must learn patience with our feeble intellects. The Writings do, however, frequently urge us to try to understand the truths of faith. In fact the whole of the Writings of Swedenborg are a clarion call to see the truth and be freed by it. Again and again they return to the theme that now spiritual darkness and ignorance are dispelled, and man is permitted—indeed urged—to enter with his understanding into the mysteries of faith—not from his self-intelligence, but from the explanations given in Divine revelation.[248]

Only the Lord can grant true enlightenment, and often man must wait a long time before little by little he comes to see some truth. But to *consent* to an important truth being an unfathomable mystery is to keep oneself in a natural faith of the memory—a faith that does not survive death. Moreover, the question matters in a practical way because it affects how man thinks and lives in all areas of life. The more he understands the relation of Providence and free will, and exactly how Providence operates, the better able he is to live a life of genuine order and use. He has to live in some manner, from some principles or others, whether consciously chosen or not. The beliefs he forms about free will and Providence go a long way toward making up his individual philosophy of living. It is a question that could not be ignored even if he preferred to remain in a state of blind faith.

XII
Then How Trust in Providence?

If we cannot have confidence that everything happens for the best, then what *can* we trust in? What good is Providence if it allows evil and harm to befall man?

In fact there is much we can trust in. If not everything happens for the best, neither does everything happen (as some believe) for the worst! Providence does govern the will of man and preserves freedom, even with the evil. The Lord seeks to turn every evil to good. No evil is permitted except that good may come from it; we can be sure that every evil has the possibility of some good resulting from it. The pages of Divine revelation—not to mention history and individual experience—offer many examples. The Lord ever bends man away from evil and towards good—never breaking, but bending. Although there is uncertainty about exactly how His government operates in regard to the time of man's death and such natural occurrences as storm and earthquake, still Divine Providence in one way or another is in every least singular of existence, and the Lord is constantly leading us towards Himself and eternal happiness. In short, while He foresees evil, He provides every good.

In other words, the Lord works continually for good in every tiniest detail, and this we should trust in. Without His infinite and universal force for good, there would be nothing. The particulars of the Lord's care of mankind almost pass beyond belief. The Writings show an incredible number of things the Lord does for us—all of which we should trust in. And we can trust that this infinite operation will never cease or be lacking in any way. Only let us not trust that the offences that come are really good; the offences are man's and they are hell.

One more important provision may be trusted in—not by all, but by those who are in good. We have already seen that the evil are given some kinds of success, and that free decisions for evil can bring harm of sorts upon others. Moreover, misfortunes of various kinds sometimes befall man from evil spirits.[249] The evil meant by "what is torn" may afflict man, through no fault of his own.[250] The evil have little assurance of protection from harm from such evils, but the Writings show that the good enjoy a protection that others lack. "All the evil which the evil intend and do *to the good* is turned by the Lord into good. . . ."[251]

In regard to worldly success with the good (but not with the evil) it is said that they receive on earth "such things as contribute to the happiness of eternal life; riches and honors for those to whom they are not hurtful; and no riches and honors for those to whom they would be hurtful. Nevertheless to these latter He gives in time, in the place of honors and riches, to be glad with a few things, and to be more content than the rich and honored."[252] The teachings on misfortune suggest that when a sphere of good prevails with man, misfortunes do not afflict him; and when the good suffer from misfortune, the purpose is that through temptation they may be led away from their evils and further into good.[253]

The good, therefore, may know that *"for those who trust in the Divine* all things advance toward a happy state to eternity, and that whatever befalls them in time is still conducive thereto."[254] "He who lives in good, and believes that the Lord governs the universe, and that all the good which is of love, and all the truth which is of faith, are from the Lord, . . . can be gifted with heavenly freedom, and together with it peace; for he then trusts solely in the Lord and has no care for other things, and is certain that all things are tending to his good, his blessedness, and his happiness to eternity."[255] It is an important assurance for the good, and the reason they can enjoy it is that "they who are in the stream of

Providence are all the time carried along toward everything that is happy, whatever may be the appearance of the means;...those are in the stream of Providence who put their trust in the Divine and attribute all things to Him ...."[256] The Lord is able to protect "all who are reformed"[257] because by life and faith they are in the stream of His Providence.

The evil can have no such assurance because they are governed by Providence, but are not in its stream. "Those are not in the stream of Providence who trust in themselves alone and attribute all things to themselves ...."[258] Frequently the Writings show that while the good are kept by the Lord in the stream of Providence such that all things conduce to their eternal happiness, the evil cannot be so protected against the hells and against themselves; although no evil is permitted unless a good may come from it, the evil tend to bring upon themselves more and more harm. The sole means of protection are Divine good and truth, and when the evil reject these, they also reject the Lord's protection. This may be illustrated by an explanation of how the Lord protects him who is being reformed:

> The good and truth which flow in through the internal render him so safe that the infernal spirits cannot do him the least harm; for that which acts inwardly prevails immeasurably over that which

> acts outwardly; because what is interior, in consequence of being purer, acts upon each and every individual particular of the exterior, and thus disposes the external to its will. But in this case there must be good and truth in the external, wherein the influx from the internal can be fixed; and in this way good can be among evils and falsities, and yet be in safety.[259]

This is said of the good, and it is clear why the evil are without the protection of which the good can be confident.[260]

The degree to which Providence can protect man, then, depends to some extent upon the man himself. "The Lord cannot protect man unless he ackowledges the Divine and lives a life of faith and charity. . . ."[261] "They who are not yet in truths are not in safety because things not true communicate with evil spirits."[262] Those in natural good only, who lack any receptacle for good and truth in the internal man, "cannot be defended by the angels" after death.[263] Thus:

> when an evil and infernal spirit assails anything Divine with intent of hurting it, . . . that evil spirit immediately deprives himself of the Lord's protection; for every spirit, the evil as well as the good, is under the Lord's protection, *and when that is taken away,* he falls into evils and falsities of every kind which are from hell, and at the same time he falls into the hands of those that are from hell, who are

> called punishers, and these then punish and torment him according to the evil that he has done or has attempted to do.[264]
>
> Every man and spirit is under the Lord's protection, the evil as well as the good; and *to him who is under the Lord's protection no evil can happen:* for it is the Lord's will that no one should perish or be punished. *But so far as anyone is under the Lord's protection he abstains from doing evil, but so far as he does not abstain he removes himself from the Lord's protection,* and so far as he removes himself he is hurt by the evil spirits who are from hell; . . . and so far as any are outside of the Lord's Divine protection, that is, so far as they do evil, they come into the power of those who do evil to them by inflicting punishment and depriving them of such things as belong to spiritual life.[265]

The evil surely feel this is unfair, and ardent democrats may complain that God discriminates against one class of men. But human concepts of justice are finite, and the Divine principle of justice is that "the Divine and its presence have for their sole end the *protection and salvation of the good . . . .*"[266]

In sum, we can trust in a government of eternal and infinite justice—not that everything is good, but that everything is governed justly, and that for those who are in good, all things conduce to their eternal happiness. This is a justice that will always result ultimately in the spiritual world, though not necessarily in this life.[267] Justice results from the judgment after death and in the life eternal. In this life society and man's actions may degenerate and grow more and more hostile to the Divine, but there will always be justice, after death surely, and on earth insofar as is possible.

Very little do the Writings say about the temporal course of the future.[268] Strong ultimate hope for the Lord's Church New Jerusalem is given, but it is not said that the world will get better and better. Some angels predicted that the civilization of Christendom would be negative to the Heavenly Doctrines, and their hopes lay with distant peoples.[269] *Last Judgment* 73 and 74 say little more than that man will be in a more free state to accept spiritual truth. This is perhaps less than we would like, but still is something important to trust in.

From many teachings about the potential of the New Jerusalem there is good reason to believe that ultimately it will extend far wider than today and influence the whole world for good more than we can imagine. Yet the real Providence and justice we should trust in are spiritual, not natural. This world is an arena for man to choose good or evil, and success or the lack thereof in this life is no criterion of true justice. To trust in Providence we must look to and think about life eternal, where all is just. If we expect too much good in this life, we are asking Providence for the wrong things. Life on earth is not a vale of tears, but neither can it be a bed of roses so long as there is evil in man.

It would be interesting to examine in detail the many ways justice *is* wrought on earth. In this life evil punishes itself often. History is full of examples of so-called poetic justice. Treachery frequently destroys the traitor, dishonesty the liar, power the powerful. Napoleon's lust of power, Charles XII's stubbornness, Hitler's racist fantasies of dominion and glory, Stalin's paranoia, French intolerance of the Huguenots in 1685, Roman Catholic decay before Luther, French hatreds during the Wars of Religion, and many more examples of apparent evil seem to illustrate the principle that evil often punishes itself readily on earth. A true concept of justice, however, must go beyond this. Trust in Providence should turn us somewhat away from the world and toward heaven and Him who is Justice itself. To turn away from the world means not to leave it, as Christian ascetics have believed, but towards spiritual use, the betterment of the spiritual state of mankind.

Genuine trust in Providence, therefore, should beware of too close an association with the idea of progress that is fashionable among many today. The happy ending syndrome of much popular culture urges that in every way things in this world are getting better and better. This is a new notion in the history of human thought. Neither ancient man nor the first Christian Church believed in unending progress in this world. The modern idea of progress emerged in the late Eighteenth and Nineteenth Centuries, after the spiritual judgment of the first Christian Church. Growing as a result of the rejection of God, it stems from the belief that if man will just take his destiny into his own hands, and ignore God, the supernatural, and written revelation, then earthly life, the only life there is, will get better and better. In their writings the greatest proponents of the modern theory of progress have been opponents of a visible God and the supernatural.[270]

Yet the heresy of purely worldly progress easily enters our thinking, influencing us away from God and eternal life. In fact to trust in Divine Providence is to trust in a spiritual justice, in this and the next life. We should trust that the Lord never ceases to love and never stops working to lead everyone to heaven, yet never destroys our freedom even if we hate Him. Just as one of the Lord's greatest temptations was to compromise man's freedom for his own good, so probably the greatest object of our trust should be that the Lord will always grant us freedom and thus life itself, including the consequences of our choices.[271]

It is concerning the subject rather than the object of trust, however, that Swedenborg's Writings present radically new doctrine. Christians for centuries believed that trust in Divine Providence centered on the actions of God, particularly His visible actions. Much New Church thought has shared this perspective. While the Writings do not neglect this outer plane of Divine operation, the most striking feature of their teaching on Providence, and especially of the work *Divine Providence,* is the emphasis on a new, more interior confidence in God: the trust that all good and all truth are from God and not from man or his own prudence.[272] The fullness of trust in Divine Providence centers less on observing deeds of God than on acknowledging that from himself man has no good or truth, and that all good and truth are from Him who is love and wisdom itself.

This acknowledgment is made formally in prayer and worship, but fundamentally, in its essence, it is made in every area of human life and usefulness, when man pursues what is good and true from God rather than what is from self. When man seeks what is good for self rather than what God reveals is good, or when he believes what his self-intelligence says is true rather than what is genuinely true, then he makes himself the source of good and truth. This principle would seem to apply not only to spiritual good and truth revealed by God, but also to moral, civil, and natural good and truth about which man must make daily decisions: always he has the choice between what he wants to be good, and what is actually good; and between what his conceit says is true, and what is actually true. Man can trust that God is genuinely the source of all good and truth only by trying to follow and live in that good and truth in every area of human endeavor. If he does this, then and only then does he have confidence in Divine Providence rather than in his own prudence, and then does God grant him the trust that various events will all benefit those who are in the stream of Providence.

Thus a full trust in Divine Providence is not something man can reason himself into. Rather it is a gift God grants if man acknowledges, by the manner of his living, that good and truth are not man's own or from self, but from God. While trust in Divine Providence should not ignore outward works wrought by God, the distinctively New Church emphasis centers on the individual looking to God for all good and truth in his life. Trust in Providence depends less on whether he accepts this or that deed as a Providential work, than on whether in his daily decisions he acts from genuine good and truth, or from his own corruptions thereof. The essential focus of trust in Providence is not external, but internal: learning to live in such a manner that one's whole life expresses the belief that good and truth are God's, not one's own. In fact the purpose of human existence is precisely this—to develop a way of life that daily trusts in Divine Providence, less by imagining how God operates in the world, than by accepting His love and wisdom as the core of our lives, as the inspiration of our every action.

These two faces of trust cannot be separated, but the internal face is primary and must precede. We cannot have confidence or light about various actions we think may be from or against Providence unless in our daily choices we accept God as the Author of good and truth. When observed events threaten confidence in Providence, the most fitting response is not to argue that evil is good, but to reaffirm the leading of God in one's own daily life. In that reaffirmation God will provide confidence and, in time, understanding.

XIII
God's Will and Man's Will in Life and History

If we could trust that Providence will make all things happen for the best, we would be deprived of much of the meaning of our lives. If every free decision we make is eternally for the best in others, then those decisions matter only for ourselves, and the life of religion becomes altogether self-centered. If Providence is the only factor in making history happen, then what is the meaning of human events?

If Providence determines all human actions, then the explanation of every event is the same: it was caused by Providence. Any apparent external cause, any apparent free will, any apparent relation of an event to other events, is irrelevant and untrue. There is relation only to Providence, and about everything that happens, we can say, that is an act of Providence. And there is nothing more of importance that need or can be said about it. (A student at Oxford once tried to answer a history examination in this way.)

If Providence is the only factor in causing human events, indeed we cannot even learn anything about Providence in human life or history. To see the operations of Providence, even tentatively, we must also be able to see the operation of man. To see how Providence operates, we must see Providence in relation to man, and so we must be able to see man. This means we must see Providence in relation to free will, since free will is what makes man to be man. To see Providence without relation to man is to see nothing. We may *know,* in that case, that Providence does all things, but we can know nothing more.

He who wishes to understand and see Providence must also understand and be able to see man, and so learn their relationship. For example, in the Seventeenth Century the dominion of the papacy threatened large parts of Germany.[273] That is man. That is free will. Providence, however, raised up King Gustavus Adolphus and others to battle the forces of the pope.[274] That is Providence, and so we can see a relation between the two. The passage cited is very instructive about how Providence operates in the affairs of religion, politics and war. It was important for the sake of the Word to check the power of the papacy, and various nations were used to this end. We see nationalism used in the service of Providence, and the use of violent means and worldly and selfish loves for the sake of eternal good. But if Providence determined everything, then the power of the papacy in Germany would also be Providence, not man's doing. And we could learn nothing about Providence except that it does everything. We would not know why Providence had to raise up Gustavus Adolphus to fight a force that was also from Providence. To learn about something, we must see it in relation to other things, not just in relation to itself. This is why if we could not see Providence in relation to man, we could learn nothing about it; we would just know that whatever happened was of Providence. Every event in life and history would have an indisputable and total explanation.

History and life would be equally meaningless to a religious person if all he saw was man and free will, and not Providence as well. This is a serious problem in today's value-free intellectual world. The only thing seen by many in life and history is man and/or society, and both life and history thus lose all transcendent meaning. What but a relation between Providence and man can make life and history mean anything of importance?

Dr. William Whitehead has called history the meeting point of the Divine will and the human will. All genuine good in human events and history is the work of the Divine will, and at the same time man's free will is granted some measure of responsibility in determining what happens in the world.

The value of the study of man is in understanding these two wills—God's and man's—and their relation in human events. To understand either one we must understand the other also. The more we understand about man, the more we can learn about how Providence leads him, foresees his evils and provides his goods. Conversely, the more we know about Providence, the more we can understand man.

History should be a source of knowledge about the Divine and the human will[275] but only if man is something that can be seen. And man can only be seen if he has free will. Where he does not have free will, we do not see man, but rather we see whatever it is that makes him do what he does. If we would know Providence, we must learn about man and about his free will.

The essential teachings for directing the study of history and society are the doctrines of the neighbor, of Providence, and of free will. Probably the easiest of these to neglect is the doctrine of free will. Truly to understand man and his past or present these doctrines must be understood together.

ENDNOTES

[1] This study was first presented in a different form to the Educational Council of the General Church of the New Jerusalem in August, 1972. In an expanded form it was presented to the Academy of the New Church as a Faculty Orientation Thesis in 1974. It was later adapted for publication in *The New Philosophy*, vol. LXXXVI (1983), pp. 4-21, 67-89, 135-148, 196-209. What follows is reprinted from *The New Philosophy* with a few editorial changes.

[2] SD 5709, 5710

[3] SD 5710

[4] DP 201, 202, 212, 285, 294:6; AE 1135:4; AC 6481-6486

[5] E.g., AC 1919:4, 5264, 6338, 6481-6486, 6490, 7007, 8478:4, 8717:2, 10774; DP 201-202, 212:2, 285

[6] DP 71, 176; TCR 475-482, 497, 498, 501

[7] E.g., DP 73

[8] TCR 463-504; DP 71-99, 138-142, 249; etc.

[9] DP 43, 97-99, 149; John 8:31-36

[10] DP 97

[11] DP 234 etc.

[12] DP 234-274

[13] E.g., DP 296

[14] DP 46-69; etc.

[15] DP 296

[16] For example, see Alfred Acton, "Divine Government and Human Freedom of Choice," *New Church Life,* Vol. XLVIII, pp. 533-557, Sept., 1928.

[17] E.g., AC 587, 3854, 3869:3, 4136:2, 4383, 5122, 6484, 10441; DP 67, 333; TCR 31; SD 4652m, 4692m, 4704, 5002; etc.

[18] See SD 4692m

[19] See DP 231:7; AR 204; AE 375:4, 1158:3; etc.

[20] See especially AC 2447, 2706, 5854; see also 4167:2; AE 683:3; SD 2713-2717; I do not believe the Writings use the word *overrule* in referring to Divine government.
[21] AC 4523f.; etc.
[22] DP 292; TCR 489; CL 444
[23] AC 25, 1255, 1874, 1992:4, 2053:2, 2180:5, 6472:2, 9334:2, 9336:2
[24] AC 1937:7, 1947, 2881, 4031, 6472:2; DP 43, 129; etc.
[25] DP 202:3
[26] Quoted in Karl Löwith, *Meaning in History*, Chicago, 1949; Phoenix edition, 1964, p. 137
[27] *Ibid.*, pp. 140, 141
[28] DP 251:3; etc.
[29] Cf. Löwith, pp. 140, 141
[30] E.g., TCR 466-502
[31] AC 10336e; cf. 4493, 5128:4, 6571:4; TCR 313, 404:2; etc.
[32] AC 8717
[33] DP 187, 189
[34] CL 523, 527-531; TCR 523; AC 9009; AE 1028; BE 113
[35] TCR 479
[36] Also see AC 944, 6481; SD 1212
[37] DP 250
[38] DP 216:2, 217, 250e; AE 1185:2, 1188:2
[39] DP 216:2; see also 217, 250; AE 1188:2
[40] AE 1185:2; see also 1189:3
[41] TCR 479; DP 249, 250; AC 6481e, 10409, 10777
[42] HH 362e
[43] HH 360:3; we are reminded of Lord Acton's maxim about power corrupting.
[44] Genesis 34
[45] AC 4493:6
[46] See AC 4493
[47] DP 243 and 251 make this point clear; cf. 278
[48] AC 4493e
[49] AC 3701:2
[50] AC 6203, 6204

[51] See also DP 281; AC 4317:5; TCR 521:2 on freedom to do evils.
[52] HD 248
[53] AC 10453:3; see also 10461, 10603, 10604; cf. 3398, 4290
[54] See especially AC 10603
[55] Matthew 18:7
[56] See AC 6487
[57] See Is. 45:7 and PP; AC 302, 1838, 1992:8, 3147:10, 4208, 6997, 7344, 8223, 9033, 10441, etc.
[58] See Exodus 4:21; 7:3; etc.
[59] 17:1
[60] HH 603:3; emphasis added; also AC 7007:2
[61] DLW 240; emphasis added; see also 247
[62] AC 6481e
[63] AC 10777; emphasis added; see also 10409:4; HD 271
[64] AC 10778: emphasis added
[65] TCR 463-504
[66] TCR 483
[67] TCR 493; cf. 592
[68] TCR 592
[69] AE 701:3
[70] TCR 483
[71] TCR 504:4; emphasis added
[72] HH 598
[73] TCR 535; emphasis added
[74] See, for example, TCR 422
[75] HH 60
[76] D. Love VI; cf. IX, XII, XIII; HH 360
[77] D. Wis. XI, Love and Charity, 4; see also DLW 335e; AE 1193, 1194, 1226
[78] DLW 251
[79] AC 4984; emphasis added; see also ISB XII
[80] AC 4984
[81] TCR 480
[82] TCR 481; see DLW 264
[83] AC 9587

[84] AC 9585; see also DLW 266
[85] TCR 494; see also 482
[86] TCR 498
[87] ISB 1:3
[88] ISB 4
[89] DLW 216; emphasis added
[90] D. Love XIII
[91] AE 1206; see 77; HH 212; CL 310; DLW 259, 268, 277-281, 316, 330, 343e; AC 1388:2, 1999, 2153, 2988:2, 3807, 3993, 4215, 4247:2,3, 5323, 5337:2, 6261, 7596; TCR 593; etc.; many examples are given of natural actions coming forth from affections of the mind. See also *Rational Psychology* 360-363, 377
[92] DLW 387; HH 60
[93] AC 4223
[94] DP 181; see also 180
[95] AC 2153, 2988, 3807, 4215, 5323, 6261, 7596; DLW 374ff., 406; AE 1206; etc.
[96] AC 5862
[97] AC 6211
[98] AC 5990
[99] AC 5990; see also HH 603:8; AC 6192; ISB 2:2, 4:3, 12, 17; etc.
[100] LJ 9; *Coronis* 19; AE 1207:4
[101] DLW 15; see 14
[102] D. Love XIXe
[103] AE 1207:3
[104] HH 315; see also DLW 167-172, 209-230, 277-281; D. Wis. VIII, 2; LJ 9, 20; AC 6077, 10634:2; AE 1206:3, 1207, 1210; SD 5709; D. Love XI:2; *Coronis* 19; and a number of other passages about the ultimate degree as the complex, containant and basis of prior discrete degrees, and as that in which the prior degrees are in their fullness and power.
[105] DLW 321e; see AC 7381:3
[106] See DLW 70; TCR 78:4; AE 628, 1219; D. Wis. VIII,3
[107] TCR 78:4; D. Wis. VIII, 2,3; XII, 5:3; LJ 9

[108] TCR 14, 103; DLW 388; DP 220:2,3; D. Wis. VIII, 3,4

[109] LJ 9

[110] AE 1086:5; see 41, 113, 328:5, 405:24, 475:17, 654:19, 666:4, 726:7, 806:3, 1087:3, 1207:4, 1226:4; HH 112; DLW 167, 168, 170, 171, 218, 298, 307, 314; ISB 12, 17; SD 4605, 4611; Canons, God, VII, 2, 3, 5; D. Wis. VIII, 2; D. Love VIII, DP 181

[111] AE 1207:4; see DLW 154, 167-169, 184, 209

[112] See *New Church Life,* Vol. LXXXVIII, pp. 335-344, July, 1968, for a fuller discussion of the relation between the civil and spiritual order

[113] ISB 11; see 10:2, 12:4, 14:4; DLW 4, 88e, 153, 163, 164, 166, 263, 315; AE 1196-1199, 1215:3, 1218; D. Wis. XIII, 5:3; *Coronis* 17:2, 19; TCR 33, 472, 473, 607:2, 154; AC 4206, 5131, 5173, 5323, 5828:3; CL 235:2; HH 567

[114] DP 190

[115] D. Wis. VIII, 3

[116] DLW 165; see also 7, 70, 160, 304, 315, 321e, 322, 340, 344, 346; D. Wis. II,3; VII, 5; VIII, 3; XII, 5:3, AC 4939, 7381:3; AE 538, 628, 1206:2, 1207:2, 1212:3, 1219, 1226:2; HH 102; TCR 78:4; compare also the teaching that the end of all things is in the spiritual sun, the causes of all things are in the spiritual world, and the effects of all things are in the natural world; DLW 134e, 154, 295e; HH 89, 567; AC 2991, 2993, 4524, 7384, 8211:2, 8812e; AE 726:4, 1197:3, 1204; CL 328; ISB 11; Canons, God, IV, 7

[117] DLW 226

[118] ISB 5; DLW 154, 226, 227; Canons, God, VII

[119] AC 7270:3; HH 303; see AC 5116:3; DLW 172; HH 9; etc.

[120] AC 4525; see 5116, 5377, 8054:2; DLW 305; HH 37 and references, 303. On the continuous connection from the First of all things created, see also *Angelic Idea;* D. Wis. XII, 5; AC 3627, 3628, 4939. Compare also the doctrine that all subsistence (or being a substance) is a perpetual standing forth. AC 3483, 3648, 4044, 4322, 4523:3, 4524, 5084:3, 6040, 6056, 6482, 9502, 10076:5, etc.

[121] See DP 78:2, 80, 108

122 HH 16
123 DP 151; see TCR 119:2
124 AC 4353e; emphasis added
125 AC 4984
126 HH 344
127 See EU 172 for another instance
128 CL 460, 502-504
129 CL 504:2; see 460:2
130 CL 54, 155
131 AC 4493
132 AC 4493
133 DP 136
134 DP 139
135 AC 10798
136 AE 1155:5; DP 96, 97; AC 2876; etc.
137 DP 139
138 DP 129:2, 136:2; AE 1155:3; to this subject we will return.
139 AE 1155:3; emphasis added
140 Inv. 6
141 DP 136:7
142 DP 130:2; emphasis added; see 150-153, 168, 219:3; AC 4110:2, 4172e, 7298:2; SD 468
143 DP 130
144 DP 136:3,4; see HD 271; AC 2842:9
145 DP 142
146 DP 136, 137
147 DP 137; see also AC 2880, 2881, 7349, 8392, 9588, 10097
148 AC 10798
149 DP 136:4
150 DP 136:4
151 AC 1947
152 AC 1937:7
153 AC 8392
154 AC 5854:2
155 AC 9588
156 AC 3854:2

[157] AC 3394e; emphasis added; see AR 427

[158] AC 7290:2; see also AC 2875, 4352:3, 2880, 4031, 4033, 5508:3, 7007:2, 8700:3, 9590, 10751e, 10777; HD 143, 148, 168; HH 293e; AE 1150:3,4; CL 208:3, where it is strongly implied that states of compulsion take place. Compare CL 298, 299, which outline steps to be followed so that a young woman's freedom may be preserved and an extorted consent to marry be avoided.

[159] TCR 318; see 320

[160] TCR 322

[161] TCR 310; such spirits and men are also called "destroyers of souls." See also AE 866:4.

[162] Recall also the example of celibates freely choosing to live unmarried at the sides of heaven—which they would not have done if they had not lived in societies favorable to celibacy. And compare TCR 446-449 on the implications of the friendship of love. The suffering caused in another by an evil friend seems to be temporary in this instance. Yet may such an interior friendship affect the type of *eternal* choices made, as well as the kind of temporary vastation after death? TCR 120:2; AC 6666e show that the presence of evil within a group tends to affect—indeed, infect—all who are in the group. See AE 1147:2.

[163] See AC 4172.

[164] TCR 579

[165] AC 4167:2

[166] AC 4211:3

[167] See also AC 4136:2

[168] AE 895:2

[169] AC 1799:2

[170] CL 339:3; emphasis added; see 130

[171] CL 340

[172] CL 341

[173] CL 348: see 345

[174] AR 618; emphasis added; compare the crucial proviso about "right education" in DP 317.

[175] *Coronis* 51:2; emphasis added; see TCR 109; AC 665, 4189, 4197:1, 4211:3
[176] See also HH 349-351, 356:3, 363, 516, 521e, 528, 535.
[177] See AC 4167:2
[178] TCR 832
[179] See CL 78, 342, 343, 348, 352; TCR 832; de Conjugio 47, 48; DP 255.
[180] CL 342:4
[181] AC 2967:2; see TCR 579
[182] Matt. 25:14-30; Luke 19:12-27
[183] AC 2967:2; see 530, 560, 649, 2284:3
[184] AC 2284:3; see 530, 660, 1906
[185] Isaiah 55:9,10
[186] DP 254:3-4; see 250:2, 326:9,10; AC 8478; HH 278, 364; SD 5790½
[187] AC 1936:4; see HH 35
[188] See AC 1974; SD 2513, 2517-2520
[189] See AR 427
[190] See AE 1226:6; AC 8719
[191] See DP 175-189.
[192] See for example W. F. Pendleton, "Notes on the Government of the Church," *New Church Life,* Vol. XVII, pp. 106-109, (July, 1897); George de Charms, *Principles of Government,* Academy Book Room, Bryn Athyn, 1960, Chapter VI pp. 60-74; W. D. Pendleton, "The Law of the Pledge," *New Church Life,* Vol. LXXVII, pp. 51-55 (Feb., 1957).
[193] TCR 494
[194] DP 287
[195] HH 543; see 581.
[196] HH 220,543; *Coronis* 15e
[197] AE 1189:4; see 1145:10,11,1164,1165.
[198] DP 296:8; emphasis added.
[199] AC 6489
[200] AC 6574:3; see also 6663.
[201] For an example, see DP 310:3.
[202] See AC 10097; TCR 490,504:5.

203 TCR 497; this teaching is frequently repeated in the Writings.
204 TCR 498:2
205 See DP 129:2, 136:2.
206 TCR 498:3; see DP 251; DLW 262.
207 AC 6204; see 6203.
208 AC 4167:2
209 TCR 498e; see AE 1164, 1165.
210 AC 6481
211 See AC 4493e.
212 DP 251
213 See AC 9354.
214 See SD 5002,5003; AC 4493.
215 See DP 252.
216 AE 1086:5, etc.; see *The Organic Unity of Man* above.
217 AC 6493; see SD 4562,4567.
218 AC 7270:4
219 See Deut. 28:1-6,8,11,12,15-24,38-42; etc.; AC 3147:10.
220 See DP 252; the fullest consideration of this subject that I am aware of is contained in the somewhat inconclusive study by Hugo Lj. Odhner, "The Doctrine of Ultimates and the Nature of Matter," published posthumously in *New Philosophy* LXXVII, pp. 127-163 (Oct.-Dec., 1974).
221 DLW 311
222 DP 187,189
223 The sin against the Holy Spirit, involving profanation and/or interior deceit, may involve such a loss of freedom; see AC 9013:6,7; 9818:27; AE 778.
224 See C. S. Lewis, *The Great Divorce.*
225 See CL 444.
226 Emphasis added; see SD 4692m.
227 See DLW 47-50; TCR 43.
228 Herbert Butterfield, *Christianity and History,* Fontana Books, London and Glasgow, 1957, pp. 124-126
229 See AC 6487.
230 See DLW 336-348; AR 888e.

[231] AC 10777
[232] DLW 202
[233] See Alfred Acton, "Divine Government and Human Freedom of Choice," address to Thirteenth General Assembly, *New Church Life,* Vol. XLVIII, pp. 533-557 (Sept., 1928).
[234] See TCR 160.
[235] DP 97
[236] DP 191-213; see also 308-321.
[237] See DP 206, 310-316.
[238] DP 19
[239] CL 444:3
[240] See DP 191-213; also 298.
[241] See AC 5952, 8516:2, 8517e.
[242] DP 210
[243] Something similar has been argued concerning man's permanent life in hell—that no one lives to eternity in hell, but he is supposed to believe he may.
[244] DP 42, 43, 158; AC 1387
[245] See TCR 109, 786; *Coronis* 51; AE 948:3.
[246] John 8:31, 32
[247] Matt. 7:12
[248] Why man should understand his faith is explained in a great many passages. For a sample selection, see *Faith* 1-4; TCR 508; AC 5432, 10659:3; AE 895, 970:1.
[249] AC 6493, 6494; SD 4562, 4567, 4758m
[250] AC 4167
[251] AC 4493e; emphasis added; see 6574.
[252] AC 8717e; see 6481, 7007; DP 215-217
[253] SD 4630m
[254] AC 8478; emphasis added.
[255] AC 2892
[256] AC 8478:4
[257] AE 1189:4
[258] AC 8478:4
[259] AC 6724:2
[260] See also TCR 614.

[261] HH 577:3
[262] AC 6769
[263] AC 5032e
[264] AE 642:2; emphasis added.
[265] AE 643; emphasis added; see 689:2, 691; described further in AC 8227, 8875, 10187; for more teachings on how the evil deprive themselves of Divine protection, see AC 2379, 3519:4, 5, 4555:2, 5036, 5893:3, 6369, 6423, 9049:6, 9141:4, 9936:2, 9962:2; HH 550; AE 472, 556b, 669, 781:12, 999:2, 1121: SD 2688, 2689, 4067.
[266] AC 8227; emphasis added.
[267] See DP 249, 250.
[268] See LJ 73, 74; AC 931; AR 547; AE 732, 764:2; TCR 109, 786-790.
[269] LJ 74
[270] See Karl Löwith, *Meaning in History,* first published by the University of Chicago, 1949; also in Phoenix Book paperback.
[271] For an interesting discussion of the temptation to remove man's freedom, see "The Grand Inquisitor" in Dostoevsky's *The Brothers Karamazov,* Book V, Chapter 5.
[272] See, for example, DP 191, 199, 201, 205-213, 310-313, 316, 318:10, 321.
[273] Inv. 24
[274] *Ibid.*
[275] See DP 187, 189.

INDEX